Living Together

Living Together

A Guide to *Counseling* Unmarried Couples

Jeff VanGoethem

Kregel
Academic & Professional

Living Together: A Guide to Counseling Unmarried Couples

© 2005 by Jeff VanGoethem

Published by Kregel Publications, a division of Kregel, Inc., P.O. Box 2607, Grand Rapids, MI 49501.

Cover design: John M. Lucas

Library of Congress Cataloging-in-Publication Data
VanGoethem, Jeff.
    Living together: a guide to counseling unmarried couples / by Jeff VanGoethem.
        p.   cm.
Includes bibliographical references and index.
    1. Unmarried couples—Religious aspects—Christianity.
2. Marriage—Religious aspects—Christianity. 3. Love—Religious aspects—Christianity. 4. Pastoral counseling.
I. Title.
BT705.9.V36 2004
259'.1—dc22   2004019277

ISBN 0-8254-3924-8

Printed in the United States of America

05 06 07 08 09 / 5 4 3 2 1

*To my wife
of twenty-five years,
Karen Sue Gladstone VanGoethem.
We never thought about cohabiting.
For us it was about marriage, love,
and a future.*

Contents

Acknowledgments | 9
Introduction | 11

Part 1: Cohabitation
  1. What Is a Cohabiting Couple? | 21
  2. How Many Cohabiting Couples Are There? | 31
  3. Why Are Couples Cohabiting? | 43
  4. The Consequences of Cohabiting:
     The Conventional Wisdom | 53
  5. The Consequences of Cohabiting: The Hard Realities | 63
  6. What Does the Bible Say About Cohabitation? | 81

Part 2: Marriage
  7. Marriage as a Covenant in the Bible | 95
  8. The Marriage Covenant in Christian History | 107

Part 3: Application
  9. Christians, Churches, and Cohabiting Couples | 127
  10. Pastoral Counseling with Cohabiting Couples:
      Two Key Principles | 143

11. Pastoral Counseling with Cohabiting Couples:
    Specific Guidelines | 157
12. Pastoral Counseling with Couples Who
    Have Cohabited | 175

Appendix A: Cohabitation Facts | 183
Appendix B: Pastoral Remarks to Cohabiting Couples | 185
Appendix C: A Sample Church Wedding Policy | 189
Appendix D: A Sample Church Wedding Ceremony:
    The Covenant of Marriage | 193

Endnotes | 197

Acknowledgments

I thank all of my teachers at Dallas Theological Seminary, beginning with those in the Th.M. program years ago. They taught me as a novice Christian how to study the Scriptures and to evaluate matters from a theological and biblical point of view, which I count a supreme gift. Since much of this material was developed in its initial form in the Doctor of Ministry program, I am deeply grateful for the help and instruction I received from my teachers in that program as well. In particular, the late Dr. David Edwards took the time to teach me the proper way of doing survey research. Dr. John Hannah invested some time in the historical aspects of this study and demonstrated great care in his comments and evaluation. Finally, Dr. James Slaughter read the material and sharpened my thinking. His comments were also very encouraging.

I am in debt to the many social science researchers who have studied the modern phenomenon of cohabitation over the last thirty years. I did no original research in that area, merely taking the time to read and study their work. I also thank the many pastors, too numerous to name here, who contributed their thoughts and experiences to this project, both in written and verbal form.

I thank, too, Larry Uphoff of Kappa, Illinois, for his help in procuring library materials in the early stages. Also, April Kinzinger helped with proofreading and corrections early on. Thank you both for being willing to help me. I also thank my faithful assistant Linda McClure, who has been a help to me in so many ways, even teaching me a thing or two in the process of developing this project.

Thank you, too, leaders and congregation of East White Oak Bible Church. What an enormous blessing you've been in my life! Thanks for allowing me some special study time now and then, without which I wouldn't have been able to complete this work. It's a privilege to serve the Lord in your midst.

Finally, I thank my devoted wife, Karen, to whom this volume is dedicated. This work would not have been possible without your patience, kindness, and thoughtfulness.

Introduction

Bob and Stacy's marriage had been volatile since day one.[1] Now, after seven years of marriage, they were headed for divorce. Neither of them really wanted a divorce but they could see no other option. Their relationship was in a desperate state, and they knew it. The first three or four years had been okay, but since then they'd grown apart and spent most of their time simmering with resentment toward one another. Although neither of them was prone to outbursts, they had hardly spoken a civil word to each other in months. Stacy had recently engaged in a foolish affair, and Bob was deeply humiliated when he discovered it. By this point in the relationship Stacy felt that she no longer loved Bob and doubted that she ever had. She realized that, from the beginning, their relationship had been based upon physical attraction more than anything else. For his part, Bob had always felt that Stacy kept her distance from him. They never really clicked. Counseling? They'd been to counselor after counselor, with little effect. To complicate matters, a child, whom they both loved dearly, had been born to them in their fourth year of marriage. All they had left was one last, not very hopeful try at counseling.

A friend advised them to see his pastor. Bob and Stacy had never been to a pastor for any kind of counseling, but in their desperation they agreed to go. They were surprised by what they heard in the first session with the pastor. After listening for a time and reviewing the history of their relationship, the pastor talked about their cohabiting for about two years prior to the marriage. No one had ever raised this point before. The pastor pointed out several statistics that demonstrated that couples who cohabit prior to marriage are far more likely to have a volatile and disruptive relationship than do couples who follow the path of traditional dating and courtship. Further, he explained some of the deeper reasons why this might be the case: cohabiting couples have less commitment to one another, a greater likelihood of unfaithfulness, less respect for one another, a greater likelihood of walking away, a feeling that one is trapped rather than liberated by the commitment of marriage. And on it went.

Bob and Stacy went home quite stunned by this new approach, but also just a little hopeful. The pastor got them to see that if they worked on rebuilding their relationship on the proper foundation, perhaps they had a chance to save their marriage. They began to sense that cohabitation had laid a poor foundation for their marriage, something they'd never considered before.

Although cohabitation is not necessarily the equivalent of a marital death sentence for couples who go on to marry, it normally and typically leads to a troubled relationship. Some people do escape this. Bill and Susie, for example, cohabited for almost ten years and finally got married in their early thirties. They're still together and recently saw their oldest child graduate from high school. Their two children are well adjusted and mature. But Bill and Susie both came from stable families. And after they got married they returned to the church, so their marriage and family were nurtured by a strong local church ministry. They made it, in defiance of the statistics, no doubt due to some of the positive steps they took once they were married.

Bill and Susie were also counseled by a pastor in the local church who was deeply committed to nurturing marriages. He helped them see that, at the time of their wedding, their background had led them to make a relatively weak commitment both to each other and to marriage. This pastor later helped them rebuild the foundation of their matrimony on a solid covenant of marriage.

Such pastoral work is a key focus of this book—helping people grasp what they may have done to themselves by cohabiting and then leading them to a better and more sound understanding of marital commitment.

All the modern research now points to cohabitation as being not likely to contribute to a successful long-term relationship. If couples are not given help in rebuilding the foundation of their marriages, it's very likely that the marriages will fail at some point. The sum and substance of this book urges pastors and others to rethink the lifestyle of cohabitation in order to help couples who have cohabited prior to marriage, who are now cohabiting, or who are considering a cohabiting relationship.

Penny and Steve raised their children in the church. Each of their four children (all sons) had come through the ranks of Sunday school, youth group, and a host of church programs. They'd all made professions of faith in Christ at one point or another and their parents felt they'd raised "pretty good" kids. One can imagine their shock when eventually not one, but two of their boys "moved in" with their girlfriends at some point during their college years. Penny and Steve reacted first with disbelief, then anger, and finally tears of despair when their sons were unresponsive in several difficult conversations.

Penny and Steve talked with their sons about morality, about faith, about doing things God's way, about what neighbors and relatives might think, and about their own example to them and the example of their grandparents and so on. Although the boys were not disrespectful, they remained unimpressed by any of this reasoning.

Their attitude was, "What's the big deal? Do you know how many kids are doing this at college? Just about everyone![2] Plus we expect to get married down the road. But look on the bright side—even if we don't get married, it's better to find out now than later that we're not suited for one another."

Penny and Steve came to feel that they lacked the arguments and knowledge to reason effectively with what they felt was a poor choice on the part of their children. Even their pastor was of little help. He sympathized with them, but couldn't offer more than what Penny and Steve had already said to their sons. Thus, *Living Together* is also written for parents like Penny and Steve who want to inculcate in their children a stronger ethic of marriage and morality than seems to be the norm in today's world. But even more, it's written for men like Penny and Steve's pastor, who should have been equipped to address this issue from a position of knowledge and conviction.

Shortly after accepting a call to his first church, a young seminary graduate, Pastor John, received a telephone call from a woman in the community who expressed a desire for a wedding. She was a stranger to the young pastor and not involved in his church. The town was very small with just a couple of churches, so options were limited for couples seeking a wedding. The pastor wanted to be "open" to these situations so he agreed to meet with her and her husband-to-be. At the meeting, the young pastor learned that things were a bit more complicated than he initially thought. This couple, in their late twenties, had been living together on and off for seven years, with several breakups and long separations, during which both had other relationships. Moreover, by now they had two small children between them.

During the interview the young woman was talkative, expressing her certainty that it was time to be married. The young man appeared to be nervous and uncertain, seldom speaking and making little eye contact with the pastor. They talked about a small wedding to be held in just two or three weeks at the vacation home of a nearby relative. The couple, particularly the young woman, pressed Pastor John to agree to perform the wedding. They didn't want any counseling or preparation. They'd been together a long time and they now just "wanted to make things right."

Desiring to be available to this couple in their time of need and also to "make things right," Pastor John agreed. After all, he much preferred them married than living together. A simple ceremony was held on a Saturday afternoon in the backyard of the vacation home. The pastor went away with some misgivings, but felt perhaps he'd built a bridge and done the right thing. On the succeeding Tuesday, however, the young woman called the pastor and said to him with obvious distress, "I think I've made a terrible mistake. After the wedding my husband took off with another woman. I don't know where he is. Is there anything we can do?"

Her intent, it became apparent, was to "undo" the wedding. As the pastor's mind raced through the implications of this new information, it occurred to him that he'd already filed the marriage license by mail. No doubt about it, this couple was married. After consoling her and trying to counsel with her, all he could tell her was, "I think you'll have to talk to a lawyer. Let me know what I can do to help you." He later heard that she quickly left the community with her children—and without her "husband."

This was a learning experience for a young, unseasoned pastor. Nothing in his seminary training had prepared him for such a scenario. Because of his inexperience, he didn't see several warning signs in this situation that, in retrospect, he realized he should have picked up on. The relationship had apparently been volatile and, also, the young man didn't seem to have his heart in the prospective marriage. Nor was this couple properly instructed and grounded in any kind of moral code. The desire to "make things right," the pastor later saw, didn't mean that things would turn out right.

The pastor also saw that he was wrong to have bypassed any in-depth premarital counseling. In whatever could have been done for this couple, he realized that his pastoral efforts had been a total failure. And who knows what damage was done to the lives involved in this sad story?

Living Together is written to help pastors like John think through how they're going to counsel and deal with cohabiting couples who get involved in the church or who seek out the church for a wedding. This very kind of scenario, in fact, first piqued my interest in the subject. I've now spent several years studying it.

Pastors and others will see the vexing premarital predicaments of cohabitation in modern American society. It's present everywhere, in families, in neighborhoods, in workplaces, and in university settings. In the present generation, perhaps as many as 50 percent of Americans have cohabited at one time or another.[3] Also, "between 50% and 60% of marriages now involve couples who have lived together."[4]

According to Michael McManus, pastors still perform three-fourths of the wedding ceremonies in the United States.[5] Thus, it is still the pastors of our land who are charged with helping most of the marriage-bound couples get ready for the commitments and responsibilities of marriage. Pastors need, then, to be prepared, much better prepared than our young friend Pastor John who was, by the way, a man of strong evangelical convictions.

Often, cohabiting couples talk to a friend or a relative before they find their way to a pastor. The fact is, given the number of cohabiting couples today and the many couples who are "at risk" or likely to cohabit, most of us sooner or later will face this issue in the circles of our families, churches, and acquaintances.

The number of cohabiting couples leads to many questions. Why are couples cohabiting? Are such couples helping or hurting their chances for a successful relationship? Why do cohabiting couples still seek out the church when they desire to be married? How does marriage differ from cohabitation? Does God have anything to say about marriage and cohabitation? How should the church respond to the modern phenomenon of cohabitation? How has this problem been addressed over the history of the church? How should modern pastors counsel a cohabiting couple? Is cohabitation, in the final analysis, bondage or bliss?

These are some of the many questions *Living Together* addresses.

Part 1 focuses on the cohabitation phenomenon, carefully analyzing what people are doing and why they are doing it. Part 2 focuses on marriage—what it is and why it is unwise to discard it or exchange it for a cohabiting relationship. In many significant ways, in fact, *Living Together* should be viewed as a defense of marriage, leaning heavily on a biblical understanding of God's ordinance of marriage. Finally, part 3 applies the information from parts 1 and 2 to those who are cohabiting, and talks to Christians, churches, and especially pastors about the lifestyle of cohabitation and what we can do about it.

Short of a glorious revival sent from heaven, I doubt we'll see the cohabiting lifestyle disappear from our midst, but perhaps we can make a difference in the lives and hearts around us. I've interviewed, surveyed, and talked to more than two hundred pastors and many other Christians and Christian leaders about this subject. I wish I could say there was one thing we could do, or one statistic we could cite, or one argument we could make that would show everyone that God's plan for marriage is better than cohabitation and that cohabiting, even with the intent of marrying later, is an untrustworthy way. Helping others come to godly conclusions on this matter will, as all experience demonstrates, prove to be an enormous challenge.

By carefully engaging the evidence and arguments of this book, however, we'll perhaps see cohabitation for what it truly is—a form of bondage that, in the end, robs people of God's best. Perhaps, too, we'll help couples understand that God's ethic of sexual purity and covenantal marriage provides the best and most likely path to the marital bliss that is universally desired.

Pastors—who are given the task across the broader church of encountering premarital couples—need to be especially convinced of these things. They need to prepare to shepherd couples in proper and godly choices prior to and in the wedding and marriage process. Pastors also need to nurture postcohabitation marriages—marriages that often need a rethinking and a rebuilding along the lines of biblical teaching. Otherwise, we'll likely see many more marital disasters. Pastors and others who counsel with cohabiting couples need knowledge, conviction, and strategies to deal with these realities. We will then have the courage and conviction to help these couples be on their way to better, more constructive, and God-honoring relationships.

PART 1

Cohabitation

Chapter 1

What Is a Cohabiting Couple?

This question may not be as easy to answer as one might think. Even the very term *cohabitation* has a widely elastic usage. Sometimes those in such a relationship are called "cohabitants." Sometimes they're called "cohabiters," sometimes spelled "cohabitors." Sometimes the term is written "cohabitaters," which supposes that "cohabitators" is possible. Finally, even the term "cohabitee" can be found. But I think we all know what is meant by the word—or do we?

So what is a cohabiting relationship?

I think we all know it when we see it: two unrelated, unmarried people who set up a household together, sharing a domestic and sexual relationship, just as if they were married. But there is more to say than this. Let me try to give a clear picture of cohabitation today.

A Definition of Cohabitation

Researchers began studying cohabitation in earnest in American society in the early 1970s. Early on it was noted that some cohabiting couples, anticipating marriage, saw their relationship as a step (usually the final step) in the courtship process. Other couples, the minority, saw their relationship as a long-term alternative to marriage. But in either case, the relationship was fully domestic, in many ways analogous to marriage.

But cohabitation differs from marriage in fundamental ways. The term *cohabitation* is kind of a cold, sociological term that sanitized earlier, not-so-nice terms such as "living in sin" or "shacking up." Despite the use of the more neutral term, at its core, both morally and legally, cohabitation is not marriage. Marriage has a social, historical, and legal weightiness that the cohabiting relationship does not have. Cohabiting couples, for example, still have very little standing in the law.[1] The American Bar Association says that under the laws of most states and communities cohabiting partners have few of the rights of legitimate "kin."[2] Many attorneys recommend that cohabiting couples draw up legal documents that spell out such things as property rights, health care directives, and other protections since these matters are not addressed in the laws of most states. It's doubtful that most cohabiting couples prepare such documents, but the legal realities seem to grasp the true nature of cohabitation. It's not marriage.

The big difference between cohabitation and marriage lies, of course, in the principle of intent. Cohabiting couples most often acknowledge that they're not married. Since ancient times, the intent to marry has been viewed as crucial in the formation of a legitimate marriage. In the modern practice of cohabitation, the intent to marry is clearly not present.

This lack of intent distinguishes cohabitation from what is sometimes called "common-law" marriage. Common-law marriages are formed without the knowledge or blessing of the legal authority that sanctions marriage (often the state or the church, depending upon the time and place). Common-law marriages were at one time more prevalent than they are today, but an increasing number of states are not recognizing them because of the complexity of sorting out whether or not a true marriage exists. But in common-law marriages, the couples involved fully intend to be married. They just don't bother with the license or the judge or the clergyman.

Cohabitation is clearly something different because the partners normally acknowledge that they're *not married* and had *no intention* to marry when they moved in together. Their intent is, in fact, *not* to be married, at least for the time being. So one thing is clear: cohabiting couples are not married.

Is there a concise definition of a cohabiting relationship? Many have been suggested. The best one I've come across is from Jackson, who states that cohabitation is "two unrelated persons of the opposite sex who share common living arrangements in a sexually intimate relationship without legal or religious sanction."[3]

Several important elements delineate a cohabiting relationship. First is the matter of *sex*. The couple is in a full sexual relationship. Second is the element of *time*. The relationship is not a casual one-night stand; rather it endures for a period of time. It's true that many cohabiting relationships begin gradually, the partners for a time maintaining their own residences, even after sharing quarters off and on. So the element of time has some "fudge" in it, but most observers look for some element of time, at least a few weeks or months before considering it genuine cohabitation.

Next is the element of a *domestic relationship*. The couple establishes a household; they live together. The extent to which financial affairs, household duties, and other traditional domestic responsibilities are carried out may vary, but a common domestic situation is established, whether it's in a university apartment complex, a house in the suburbs, or an old shack down a rural dirt road. The final element is that important matter of *intent*. Clearly the cohabiting couple intends not to marry; cohabiting couples are often, in fact, acutely aware that they are not married. Couples who draw up special legal agreements to govern their relationship often include strong language about the impermanence of their relationships. So cohabitation is specifically, purposefully, and fundamentally *nonmarital*.

Often someone may state about a cohabiting couple, "They're married in the eyes of God." This less than thoughtful analysis overlooks the very nature of the relationship. However the couple has come to be in their cohabiting condition, they've decided specifically *not to marry*. In fact, one intriguing study cited later in this chapter shows that cohabiting couples actually bear more resemblance to single people than to married people.

Patterns of Cohabitation

At the age of fifteen, Mark was devastated by his parents' divorce. In his young mind there seemed no good reason for it. An only child, he was loved by both of his parents. They were involved at his school functions, they came to his sporting events, they showered him with attention every step of the way. Raised in a prosperous home with both parents college educated and in successful careers, Mark lacked for nothing growing up.

His parents didn't seem to fight that much. Sure they were somewhat cold to each other at times, but he couldn't understand the divorce. It was not until years later that Mark discovered the real reason: his father had found someone else. Mark was shielded from this at the time of the divorce.

Brokenhearted, Mark, over the years, grew more deeply disillusioned about marriage. He became convinced that it was unnatural to expect two people to stay together for life. One of his university professors reinforced this viewpoint. Now in his late twenties, Mark has had three cohabiting relationships, the longest of which was four years. He still hopes for that elusive long-term relationship, but still without any intention of committing to marriage.

Mark cohabits because of a philosophical mind-set—he really does not believe in marriage. He doesn't view a period of cohabitation as a final step in the courting and dating process; he views it as an end in itself, as an alternative to marriage. More and more people in our society think this way, particularly those who've been marked by divorce, either their own or that of someone close to them.

Tina and Brad met in the tenth grade, and they had their first date that same year. They began going with one another not long after. By their senior year in high school they were sexually intimate and had discussed marriage. They knew they loved each other, but they wanted to wait to marry until Tina finished her education. An outstanding student, she received a nice scholarship to a nearby state university. Brad went to work and in time moved out on his own. After a couple of years of college, Tina moved in with Brad. By now they were engaged to be married, Tina sporting a very nice diamond ring. Thus, a wedding date was set to coincide with Tina's graduation. Both sets of parents accepted the live-in arrangement, Tina pointing out to them that it was a lot cheaper—they could save a lot of money for a wedding and honeymoon if they shared expenses.

Tina and Brad are another kind of cohabiting couple, one who views living together as the final step in the courtship process. Marriage is in the picture the whole time and the cohabitation takes place with pragmatic purposes in view, like sharing bills. With a decrease in the stigmas against living together, it's become much more common for couples to make this sort of arrangement.

Alice and Hans moved in together after a few wild and exciting dates. Their relationship proceeded very quickly to sex and then to cohabitation. Alice had it in her mind that she was going to marry this exciting man, who was from another country and culture. His accent intrigued her and she found him very desirable. Hans, on the other hand, wasn't so sure about marriage. He was perfectly willing to move in with Alice; he liked her a lot, but he needed to know a lot more about her before getting serious about marriage. Most of these thoughts were not discussed until long after they'd moved in together.

In time, things went bad between them. Arguments and misunderstandings plagued them, and Hans began to display a violent temper. One day he struck Alice, bloodying her lip. In retaliation she pressed charges and Hans found himself in a lot of trouble. They eventually went their separate ways, albeit with both emotional and physical scars.

Hans and Alice are in the category of couples who cohabit to test their relationship, particularly as we think about it from Hans's point of view. Marriage is in the picture but it's not at all a certainty. The couple, or at least one of the partners, reserves the right to end the relationship if things don't work out as anticipated. This couple also shows the tremendous misunderstandings and misconceptions that can develop if the nature of the cohabiting relationship is not clarified at the outset.

A college student I knew, for example, moved in with his girlfriend his last year of college. I asked him if he thought they'd get married. He said, "I don't know. I think so. We haven't talked about it that much." After graduation he and his girlfriend were both offered good jobs, but in different parts of the country. They took the jobs and just drifted apart.

Different patterns of cohabitation reflect the different reasons why couples move in together. Researchers have tended to settle on three kinds of cohabiters who make up the majority of such couples. Some in a cohabiting relationship view their condition as an alternative to marriage. It may be a long-term arrangement or not long at all, but marriage is not in view. They have no moral problems with cohabitation and may even view marriage as an impediment to a good relationship. Other couples are on the way to marriage and live together in the final stage of their courtship, perhaps just for a few weeks or months, perhaps much longer. But they intend to marry and often do. Finally are those couples who use the cohabiting period to "test" their relationship to see if they're suitable for the deeper commitment of marriage. Sometimes it's a genuine "test" and other times it may be done with less seriousness and sincerity.

Sometimes cohabiting couples go through periods or stages in their own understanding of what their relationship means. Researchers have found that the partners frequently do not agree on the nature of their relationship. This is one of the deep problems of the cohabiting lifestyle.

Anyone trying to give counsel to a cohabiter would be wise to seek clarification on what his or her motivation for cohabiting actually is. There may be deep hurt at the root, as in the case of Mark, or there may be careless decision making as in the case of Hans and Alice. And the partners themselves may not fully agree on what the nature of the relationship is.

When meeting cohabiting couples, it would be of interest to ask them what kind of cohabiting relationship they have. Are they on the way to marriage? Is their arrangement a rejection of marriage? Are they trying each other out for marriage? Are they on the same page together regarding the nature of their relationship? The studies vary but it's safe to estimate that about 50 percent of cohabiting couples do go on to marry one another. The proportion of first marriages that were preceded by cohabitation increased from 8 percent during the 1960s to about 50 percent in the 1990s.[4] The number of cohabiting couples going on to marry is now decreasing, however, perhaps signaling a further decline in how marriage is viewed by many in our culture. More and more people like Mark don't want to get married and see cohabitation as an acceptable alternative. In the 1970s, for example, two-thirds of cohabiting couples went on to marry within three years. Now the rate is half of that.[5] An implication of this decline is relevant as we seek to counsel with cohabiting couples; we need to determine into which category the cohabiting couple we have before us falls.

One of the problems of cohabiting relationships is that men often enter it with less intention to marry than do women. The reverse could be true in a given situation, but research has shown that it is the women who are more often disappointed. Johnson says, speaking primarily about college students,

Most females really believe they are going to marry the guy. . . .
They will tell you . . . "We're gonna get married. We love each other.
This is just sure to work." The young men responded and their
number one reason for cohabitation was readily available sex. It had
nothing to do with marriage.[6]

The girl thinks the relationship is headed for marriage; the guy
emphatically disagrees. Some men, in fact, deeply disrespect the
women with whom they cohabit. They view them as "easy," not at
all the kind of faithful women they'd like to marry. We'll revisit this
point again, but it's necessary at this juncture to state the obvious—
it's easy for a woman to get used in a cohabiting relationship. The
double standard is alive and well, and brings into focus something
that our grandmothers might have said: "Why would you buy the
cow if you can get the milk for free?" This advice might seem old-
fashioned, but it's unwise for a young woman (or any woman for that
matter) to give herself to a man without the commitment of marriage. As one researcher said to women thinking about cohabiting,
"If you want someone to marry, choose someone who *won't* live with
you" (emphasis his).[7] Although the claim has engendered controversy,
many researchers have stated that women, more often than men, are
hurt by the failure of a cohabiting relationship.

Here we discover the first fault line that cracks the cohabitation
lifestyle. The nature of the cohabitation relationship may undermine
the future togetherness of the couple and lead to disruption either
before or after marriage. Misunderstandings, unequal levels of commitment, nonparallel philosophies, and other complexities make these
relationships much less likely to succeed than, say, two people in love
who look forward to marriage, maintain their sexual purity, and come
together in the liberation of conventional marriage. It is thus important for pastors and others who counsel with cohabiting couples to
press the point, particularly with women, that one's partner may not
possess the same view of their relationship. This disparity in percep-

tion, commonly present in cohabiting couples, often seriously undermines the health of the relationship. The nature of the cohabiting relationship is a decision *not* to marry. It's important to not miss this point—it changes things at the very foundation of the relationship. Rindfuss and VandenHeuval have argued quite persuasively that cohabitation ought not to be studied from the point of view of marriage, but rather from the point of view of singleness.[8] Their study displayed that in such matters as child-rearing responsibilities, career, home ownership, and self-identification, cohabiting people resemble single people more than they resemble married people. They propose that cohabitation be viewed, in fact, as a way of prolonging singleness. On a philosophical level, the authors of the study state that cohabitation springs out of the individualism of American culture. And singleness reflects the true character of cohabiting couples—they typically do not have a joint bank account, they don't buy property together, they don't list one another as beneficiaries on insurance policies, and so forth. They maintain their singleness.

In many cohabiting relationships, an atmosphere of uncertainty and indefiniteness hovers about the relationship. In many cases cohabitation might better be seen as a living arrangement for individuals not prepared to make the marital commitment. A given couple may go on to marry but it may take a long time for them to reach that point. And in many cases, the relationships do not survive to that point. It is thus not surprising that many of these unions do not last long and those that do go on to marriage seem to form a much more volatile and fragile union. Since, then, cohabitation is actually a way of prolonging singleness, how can it be thought of as a sound way to prepare for marriage?

When disruption does occur in the relationship, whether before or after marriage, what happens to the hearts and souls of those who experience the breakups? Johnson states,

Cohabiting couples . . . do not want to be committed. They want it where they can get out pretty easy if they want to. Easy to walk out the door. You will find out how hard it is to deal with that.[9]

He points out that when a cohabiting relationship ends, it can be quite devastating. In his own experience, he cohabited with a woman he later married. But the union was unstable and fraught with problems. Even though they had a child, his wife decided to leave and he said it hurt "like hell."[10] Moreover, few networks provide help and support for former cohabitants. There are Divorce Care groups and Single Again groups, but who ever heard of a Cohabiting fall-out ministry?

That there are problems inherent in cohabiting relationships is becoming clear. Later in this book, much more will be said about that. But the next important question is just how much cohabiting is occurring today?

Chapter 2

How Many Cohabiting Couples Are There?

To state the obvious, cohabiting relationships have "gained widespread acceptance over the last twenty-five years."[1] Many years ago the famous American sociologist Margaret Mead saw this coming trend. In the 1960s Mead had grown disappointed over the American custom of dating. Anticipating the rise of cohabitation, she proposed, perhaps somewhat idealistically, that a "two-stage" marriage would emerge. The first stage, licensed separately from the second, would involve serious commitment, but would require that the couple not have children. The second stage, the parental stage, would follow only if the couple wanted to continue their relationship and if they wanted to have children.[2] Mead seemed stuck somewhere between the older, more traditional world of those who courted and married, and the newer, more novel world of those who just moved in together.

But she wasn't that far off the mark. She just failed to anticipate how attitudes would change so rapidly so as to allow couples to simply move in together without the serious commitment she envisioned.

Although developments didn't occur just as Mead predicted, the "try-it-before-you-buy-it" approach to marriage is, nonetheless, common today.

So, how much cohabitation currently occurs, and what are the trends and implications? This chapter illuminates the modern practice of cohabitation in the United States by citing relevant figures and studies that cover the last twenty-five years. The statistics demonstrate that cohabitation has become a powerful reality in the modern world.

The Early Days

Candy and Morris were hippies. They "dropped out" and "turned on" back around 1970—dropped out, as in dropped out of college and turned on, as in toward each other. Amid the rebellion against traditional morals that infected young people in those days, Candy and Morris moved in together when it was still called "shacking up." At that time, cohabiting was much more novel than it is now. Their respective families reacted with horror at yet another demonstration of behavior they felt was beyond any reasonable propriety. Candy and Morris eventually married and, defying the statistics, went on to have a stable marriage. They look back on their experience of cohabiting and shake their heads at the wrath and shock it once aroused. These days it's not a big deal.

A little history offers some perspective on this blasé outlook. The earliest information in print on modern cohabitation first emerged around Candy and Morris's time. Most of this information was not scholarly research, but rather attempts in magazines and papers to capitalize on a novel lifestyle that more and more people were trying. It was interesting stuff. The earliest true research was on college students in the early 1970s and very few broad conclusions could be drawn because of the small scale of the studies. Reading this material with thirty years of hindsight, though, helps explain the early enthusiasm with which cohabitation was greeted by many researchers and scholars. They seemed to believe that they'd stumbled onto something that was bound to benefit many in American society. One frequently reads, for example, that in these early cohabitation situations, predications were made about the helpfulness of cohabitation for future marital stability. This was the birth of what I call the "conventional wisdom" on cohabitation, and it prevailed in American society for many years. Much of this early gushing has now been, as we shall see, dashed upon the rocks of reality.

Later Research

There was no doubt, however, that a trend was discovered. Even as early as 1970 the rate of cohabitation was shown to have increased eightfold since 1960. By 1980 the increase was again profound. Raw figures indicate that the number of cohabiting couples increased from 523,000 in 1970 to about 1.6 million in 1980. In a fourth of these relationships children were present.[3] Further, almost all researchers consider cohabitation rates conservative estimates since important populations, such as college students, are seldom included in the studies. Also, some people are reluctant to admit they're cohabiting when poll takers ask them about their lifestyle.

Through the 1980s the cohabitation rate showed no sign of leveling off. By 1981, 1.8 million couples were cohabiting, an increase of 14 percent in just one year. In 28 percent of cohabiting situations, children were present, and the number of couples cohabiting at any one time had grown to its highest rate—4 percent of the national population.[4] Also during the 1980s, researchers discovered that the rates of cohabitation were even higher when calculated on the younger population. In the population of those cohabiting in 1981, for example, two-thirds of the men and three-fourths of the women were under thirty-five years of age.[5] By 1986 the number of cohabiting couples had surged to 2.2 million and by the time the decade ended cohabitation expert James Sweet was able to state that "nearly half of persons entering first time marriages . . . have cohabited prior to marriage, most of them with the person that they married. And well over half of persons who remarry live with a partner between their marriages."[6]

Scholars also show that the so-called decline in the marriage rate over these years (the number of people getting married in a given year) is actually offset by cohabitation. In reality, young people today are setting up house as early and as often as they ever did, but without the benefit of marriage. Some observers have concluded that the importance and significance of marriage has simply declined in our culture, and cohabitation has begun to take its place. Perhaps we haven't yet seen the peak of the cohabitation phenomenon. If this is true, it likely doesn't bode well for the future of our nation.

Substantial rises in rates of cohabitation were again seen in the 1990s. It is of interest that the rates rose in every age group. One study in the early 1990s indicated that in the span of the normal age of marriage—between ages twenty-five and thirty-four—between 20–24 percent of all unmarried adults were cohabiting.[7] Research in the 1990s also indicated that cohabiting relationships were breaking up more frequently than in the past. By the end of the 1990s it was determined that perhaps 5 percent of the population was cohabiting at any given time and nearly half of the people marrying for the first time had cohabited at one time or another.

The most recent information, based on the 2000 census, indicates that by the year 2000 the number of cohabiting couples in the U.S. had grown to over 4.7 million, an increase of more than ten times the number in 1960. More than half of all first marriages are now preceded by cohabitation, and more than one third of cohabiting-couple households have children present.[8] An accompanying hardening of attitudes is evident on the part of some concerning the favorableness of cohabitation. Forty-four percent of single men in their twenties agree with the statement, "I'd only marry someone if she agreed to live together first." One-third of men in this category state they are cohabiting or have cohabited at one time.[9] It is ironic, though, that many young men are more adamant than ever about the desirability of cohabiting prior to marriage at a time when the evidence against the wisdom of doing so is at last becoming clear.

Whitehead and Popenoe have provided the summary below of the growth in cohabitation rates:[10]

Year	Number (in millions)
1960	.439
1970	.523
1980	1.589
1990	2.856
2000	4.736

George Barna pointed to the implications of these statistics and the accompanying relaxed attitudes about cohabiting. Young people anticipating marriage today, Barna states, may be the first generation of Americans to feel a total confusion regarding marriage, a confusion caused by the conflict of today's prevailing cultural values. On one side they hear parents and other authority figures proclaim the value of marriage while on the other side they see our culture condoning and—in many cases—practicing an alternate path.[11] Increased cohabitation rates and an even shakier confidence in marriage may well be in our future.

Every year I teach a workshop for all the couples anticipating marriage in our church. Over the years I've seen an increasing fear in the eyes of the participants as they contemplate marriage. There's too much divorce, too much disruption in relationships, and young people are consequently afraid of marriage and commitment. I don't recall these feelings when I was twenty-one years old and preparing to marry. I looked forward to marriage, and cohabiting was never once considered. I didn't believe I had to "try out" my wife-to-be to make sure that our marriage would work. And I knew that she felt the same way. But it's a different ball game today.

Characteristics of Cohabiting Couples

More is yet to be learned about the attitudes of those entering cohabiting relationships today. Some fairly well-recognized generalizations can be made about those who enter cohabiting relationships, and although the following observations are generalizations, they suggest what tends to be present in the attitudes and thoughts of cohabitants. They are, however, by no means hard and fast rules, and it would be wise to search out the background and attitudes of each cohabiter with whom we come in contact.

Cohabitants are likely to have less religious commitment than those who do not cohabit. Further, among marginally religious people who cohabit, their level of religious participation tends to decrease, while among individuals who marry it tends to increase. This has obvious implications for pastors. People tend to take a hike from the church when they embrace the cohabiting lifestyle, but they might be ripe to win back when they decide to marry.

Cohabitation has always been more characteristic of lower socioeconomic groups than higher socioeconomic groups. Despite the attention given to university settings and the cohabitation rates of college students, higher levels of cohabitation often exist among the lesser educated segment of the population. Thus, even pastors in small towns and rural areas—where educational levels may tend to be lower—see a high number of cohabiting couples in their communities.

Cohabiting couples also indicate that at times they do struggle with the morality of their choice to live together outside of marriage. Such appears to indicate that a moral code lies in the hearts and minds of at least some of those who cohabit. Thus, an appeal to morality may not be a bad idea when counseling with cohabiting couples.

In what has become well known to researchers, cohabitants betray more liberal attitudes regarding divorce, premarital sex, and sexual unfaithfulness. Today, only about one-quarter of unmarried adults view cohabitation as morally wrong and another fourth have some "moral qualms" about it.[12] In probing the moral sensibilities of couples involved in a cohabiting relationship, I often find a certain honest unease about it but also some defensiveness. I've raised the question with cohabiting individuals, "Can you trust someone to be faithful to you after you marry that person if he or she didn't have enough moral fiber to marry you without a season of cohabitation?" Cohabiting couples often talk about the "committed relationship" they're in. This seems like soap opera talk. Committed to what? One writer stated that "living with your boyfriend is fun. It is also practical, meaningful, and a sign of deep commitment."[13] I can follow the logic of someone who states that cohabiting is "fun" and even "practical," but the logic eludes me when it's stated that cohabiting is "meaningful" and "a sign of deep commitment." Everything we're learning about cohabitation argues that the relationships tend to lack weightiness and by definition tend not to result in long-term commitment.

It appears that cohabitation has evolved over the last few decades from something called "living in sin" to something accepted by modern society. The link between marriage and sex has certainly been broken. But is this relaxing of moral attitudes a good idea? As with many of the moral choices being made today, the ensuing consequences prove that the choices lacked God's wisdom.

Linda Waite and Maggie Gallagher published a book challenging the idea that cohabitation is a good idea.[14] The book is only partly about cohabitation, but it shattered many of the common politically correct myths, causing Harvard University Press to refuse publication based upon what appeared to be political reasons.[15] We need, however, to examine some of these myths. Waite has presented evidence arguing for the superiority of marriage over singleness, divorce, cohabitation, and all forms of marital instability.[16] She cites studies demonstrating that in the areas of health, longevity, material well-being, sexual and emotional satisfaction, consequences for children, and other categories, married people are better off. Other sociologists have chimed in to report that marriage is a guardian against poverty, lower educational achievement, poor psychological health, children's marital failures, and so on. It's clear, then, that marriage secures a more favorable future for most children and families.

The long-term commitment of marriage is what allows partners in marriage to "make choices that carry immediate costs but eventually bring benefits."[17] Cohabitation, on the other hand, surrenders in particular those benefits associated with long-term commitment. Rather than being constructive for the individual, cohabitation diminishes the individual because each partner is limited in what he or she can contribute to the other. Whether in the pooling of finances or something like the investment of time in family traditions, the cohabiting person is less likely to invest in the other person and is more likely to remain focused primarily on caring for himself or herself. It's simply more risky and somewhat contradictory for cohabiters to invest in the relationship. Married couples, however, find investment in the long-term aspects of the relationship natural and safe. This failure of cohabitants to invest resources in the relationship creates another fault line in the foundation of cohabitation.

The proven failures inherent in cohabitation raise the hope that the social forces at work in the increasing instances of cohabitation will be reexamined. Waite observes that social scientists have a "responsibility to weigh the evidence on the consequences of social behavior in the same way as medical researchers evaluate the evidence on cigarette smoking or exercise."[18]

Where, then, are our teachers and prophets? If nowhere else, they'd better be in the pulpits of our land.

Writing a column published by the Scripps Howard News Service, Terry Mattingly lamented that few pastors seem willing to address the problem of cohabitation from the pulpit, despite its widespread practice across the land. Michael McManus, who is active in Marriage Savers, a ministry to married couples, often asks groups he speaks to this question: "How many of you have ever heard a sermon on cohabitation?" He claims he never sees more than one or two hands raised.[19] Do pastors not realize how many people are living together outside of marriage? Are they afraid to preach God's Word on this subject? One would hope not, especially since the broader culture signals day after day that couples need not hesitate to move in together. Have some churches and pastors even reached the point of ceasing to believe that cohabitation is a form of sexual sin? It seems the least pastors can do about this issue is thunder God's truth from the pulpit.

Jenkins wrote the following for a British audience but it applies no less across the ocean, right here in the United States:

> If Christians, if the church, sincerely believe that marriage, compared with living together, is a superior product, then we must really make an effort to "sell" it to our increasingly secular nation. In a world where more and more people have sincere doubts about whether marriage is really a good idea at all, we need to develop a convincing biblical apologetic for marriage. We need to be in the business of persuading people that marriage is good, from God, and is best. And when we have persuaded them we need to do everything we can to help them build strong, successful marriages.[20]

In the April 29, 1997, issue of *Newsweek,* columnist Jonathan Alter penned an open letter to Madonna upon the birth of her child. She produced this child prior to her current marriage with her boyfriend and cohabiting partner at that time, Carlos Leon. Alter took exception to Madonna's announcement that she and Leon would not be getting married. Alter first reacted with sarcasm: "How conventional! How predictable! How uncool! You've now joined celebrities like Farrah Fawcett, not to mention nearly a third of the rest of the country." He then began to chastise her for the philosophy or attitudes that apparently governed her decision making. He mocked her rationalization that "years spent living with Carlos under the same roof without being married would be better for the child than if a forced wedding gave way to a predictably messy Hollywood divorce." Alter cited her apparent belief that she did not need a man, which he claimed is an "extraordinarily destructive view." He exhorted her to read up on the problems of single-parent families and warned her about the example she was setting for others. Alter, the married father of three, seemed particularly disturbed by Madonna's apparent casual disregard for marriage. Finally, he cited research showing that for all its flaws, marriage is still what leads people to responsible and constructive behavior. He appealed to her to at "least speak up for the idea [marriage], the way you speak up for tolerance, sexual freedom, and artistic expression." In the end, Alter appealed to common sense, telling Madonna that "you understand the significance of contracts. They impose reciprocal responsibilities that make completing a project . . . easier. . . . But the bond itself is more than a piece of paper. It's a measure of . . . commitment." He ended on a positive note by lecturing this famous idol that "the next wave is restoring the family, and with it, the country itself. Ride it, Madonna." The title of the essay? "Get Married, Madonna."[21]

More voices like this are sorely needed. And perhaps Alter's optimistic assessment will prove to be correct. Perhaps the next wave will be a return to marriage and family. Many of us would certainly welcome such a development. But in the meantime, it must be emphatically stated that people who believe God's Word must not give in to the culture on the issue of cohabitation, but rather be part of that chorus of voices, however few, who say *get married!* But we must also provide the biblical and reasoned arguments that so many need. Who knows, maybe the tide is turning. Madonna herself has since gotten married! For now, it's enough to conclude that over against cohabitation marriage provides a greatly enhanced opportunity to build a successful life. But more attention must be given to recovering the proper view of marriage. First, though, it would be enlightening to study the reasons that people are so likely in our times to enter a cohabiting relationship.

Chapter 3

Why Are Couples Cohabiting?

L arry and Barb lived up the road from me a number of years ago. I didn't know them well but I'd greeted them and exchanged pleasantries a few times. I thought they were married, but actually they'd been in a long-term cohabiting relationship for about twenty years. One day I was sitting in my study at church and Barb called me. She told me that Larry had been killed the day before in an accident, and that she needed a funeral and a preacher. They didn't have a church home, she said, so she called me. I talked with her, working out the funeral plans, and during the conversation discovered that Barb and Larry had never been married. In a subsequent conversation, I worked up the nerve to ask her why. They'd been together all that time, had children together, and so forth. Barb paused a minute and then said, "You know, I don't really know why we didn't get married. We talked about it a few times. We had nothing against getting married. It was just procrastination I guess."

That's a lot of procrastinating! Twenty years' worth, through children, a life together, and finally death. Barb was, understandably, very sad about it all, and I sensed her deep regret. Why, though, do people move in together apart from marriage? What factors and reasons form the foundation of this philosophy of living? What influences and attitudes mark cohabiting couples? Do couples always know with utter clarity what their motives and reasons are? Are the reasons and steps to the cohabiting lifestyle always carefully and logically thought through? The analysis offered in this chapter is presented in generalizations, but chances are, a given cohabiting couple will represent a mixture of the following reasons that have typically led to cohabitation.

According to research, the most frequently cited reason for cohabitation is to ensure compatibility with a potential spouse. The next most cited reason is economics—living together can drastically lower living expenses for two people who are "together," sexually intimate, and have no moral constraints regarding cohabitation. Other significant reasons include a desire to retain independence, a desire to avoid long-term commitment, and greater sexual freedom.[1] Many people today have embraced these reasons, which amount to what could be termed a cultural prejudice against marriage. It may not have occurred to these couples how out of joint it is, given the history of the human race, to adopt a prejudice *against* marriage. While many cohabiters may be unsure about why they are cohabiting, even more are unsure about the commitment of marriage.

Ambivalence and Ambiguity

Many people in cohabiting relationships may not, like Barb, be able to clearly articulate why they entered into a state of cohabitation. Ambivalence and ambiguity may cloud their own minds. Some of the modern research on cohabitation documents that many people enter into cohabiting relationships gradually and without clear goals. Many couples do not make a well-thought-out, thoroughly discussed decision. Rather, they sort of drift together as a result of sexual intimacy and spending increasing amounts of time together.[2] The couple might begin by spending some nights together until one of them finds it more convenient to move some clothes and personal belongings to the home of the other. In time, the former residence is left behind altogether. As a consequence of this happenstance, cohabiting couples often have conflicting goals and expectations about their own relationships.

One early study in 1984 focused on the question of how cohabiting couples introduce one another in various social settings.[3] Such couples often find introductions awkward, many choosing to keep their roles vague when introducing and referring to the other. They offer just first and last names perhaps, and no explanation of the relationship. Even couples having a lengthy period of cohabitation will handle introductions in this way. Sometimes one will hear the word "girlfriend" or "fiancé," but more often than not, these terms are not used, since they may not exactly fit the circumstances. Using the terms "girlfriend" or "boyfriend" may not seem "weighty" enough. They are, after all, sharing living quarters. And the term "fiancé" may be utterly inappropriate for many couples. So the ambiguity that exists in many of these relationships finds itself into the very vocabulary of those cohabiting.

Some couples who cohabit are, of course, clearly in a marriage preparation mode. So some are spared this vagueness and ambiguity, but many are not. It's important, then, to sort out intentions and relationship status when thinking together with a couple about their decision to cohabit. Is it really wise for cohabiters not to discuss with one another such issues as responsibilities, obligations, future goals, and marriage? Books are being published today urging cohabiting couples to enter into written contracts that spell out property rights, bill-paying responsibilities, rules for debt-encumbrance, inheritance issues, and other practical concerns.[4] Doesn't a failure to agree on the nature of the relationship increase the risk of misunderstanding, disappointment, and heartbreak? Marriage tends to eliminate many such concerns, since both parties understand exactly what they're committing themselves to.

Sexual Liberty

The opportunity for sexual love apart from marriage is clearly at the heart of cohabitation. Some have tried to diminish the importance of this motive by arguing that at least cohabiters are not practicing promiscuity. Cohabitation does imply at least some sexual restraint and some level of faithfulness within the relationship. Yet most researchers trace the phenomenon of modern cohabitation to the sexual revolution and the historic changes in dating and sexual practices among unmarried people. As mentioned in previous pages, the rise of cohabitation coincided with not only the rising age of couples at the time of marriage, but also with increased sexual freedom among the unmarried. These social trends are well established.

Research also shows that cohabiting couples express more liberal views on matters regarding sex. Evidence can be marshaled to show that the average cohabiting couple will not have the same views on sexual morality as, say, a biblically informed pastor or church member. Sexual permissiveness, then, is a key factor in understanding cohabitation. One university coed I talked to not long ago told me that she was already on her third cohabiting relationship in her first two years of college. Most likely, these relationships involved little more than convenient sex. The moral code—the old-fashioned moral fiber and moral commitment—in the area of sex and marriage evident in the lives of our grandparents is simply not present in much of today's youth. It's not surprising, therefore, that sexual unfaithfulness is a greater problem among those who are or who have cohabited than among those who enter marriage the more traditional way.

Cultural Influences

A person in a cohabiting relationship may have accepted much of the modern thinking that has infiltrated our modern culture. The so-called sexual revolution and the devaluing of children in our industrialized, urbanized, and modernized society have "diminished the need for marriage."[5] Cohabitation fits the individualism of the times, the emphasis on pleasing oneself, and the de-emphasizing of commitment to others. Cohabitation is no longer considered an issue of sin and morality. Jenkins identified this mind-set remarkably well in the following paragraph:

> Cohabitation has become respectable. The average couple is not consciously rebelling against marriage when they move in together. They are just doing what everyone else is doing. They are following a social norm in just the same way as their parents did when they got married without having first lived together. . . . The increasingly social acceptability of living together creates a sharp difference in perception between the church and the couple. . . . To the couple their decision to marry, far from being a sign of remorse or repentance, is in fact a vote of confidence in cohabitation. The experiment has been a success. Living together has worked and marriage is the final seal of approval on their relationship. The church may wish to speak of sin; they have no concept of sin. The church may be looking for signs of repentance: they have never considered that anyone could consider living together actually to be wrong (providing you are in love).[6]

It's clear that the cultural influences of our times have engendered new and different attitudes, which have had a powerful impact on the question of marriage and cohabitation. The result may be that many unmarried people believe that finding a partner for life is an unrealistic expectation. They may long for such a thing, but believe it's next to an impossibility and settle for whatever a more temporary relationship will give them in the present. Such is the consequence of a "marriage-hostile culture."[7]

There's an increasing awareness of the value of marriage, however, and that our lengthy experiment with cohabitation and other living arrangements has done nothing but contribute to costly cultural decline. Still, even public policies—for example, the elimination of the so-called marriage tax—have failed to create stronger incentives for marriage. Currently, our federal government and some state governments are struggling with the question, "Should the government encourage marriage?" The state of Oklahoma, for example, has developed an initiative to encourage marriage and prevent divorce, funding a myriad of programs designed to get people married and with the proper preparation. President George W. Bush has said, "Strong marriages and stable families are incredibly good for children, and stable families should be the central goal of American . . . policy."[8]

Critics call such policies "big-government social engineering," but government has, in fact, recognized the cost to society in the diminished ethic of marriage. Our local, state, and federal governments spend billions on enforcing child support, adjudicating custody issues, and on other services that are necessary because people don't get married or don't stay married. One participant in a government-sponsored Oklahoma program was able to understand that the boyfriends she'd been seeing did not measure up to husband material and planned to be more careful about who she would eventually marry.[9] Wouldn't it be wonderful if we've entered a period in our cultural development that moves back toward marriage, stable families, and moral commitment?

Many among us, however, like many cohabiting couples, possess a hodgepodge of prevailing, individualistic cultural views that distort marriage to the point of dismissing altogether the importance of matrimony. Those of us seeking to rebuild an ethic of marriage and sexual purity thus face an uphill battle.

Economics

Economic concerns are the most pragmatic of the forces driving the cohabitation lifestyle. A couple dates, they get sexually involved, and they find themselves spending a great deal of time together, including many nights. Sooner or later it dawns upon them that they can do what they're doing much cheaper by sharing a residence and other living expenses. Their thinking has severed the moral connection between sex and marriage so the economic aspect of their relationship becomes the dominant consideration. I've heard numerous couples say, "We just can't afford to live apart."

This practical element of cohabitation reinforces more important cultural trends such as starting families later and having smaller families. Since young people, especially, are not yet concerned with having and raising children, cohabitation is a more convenient choice. Young people see, too, an advantage in the trend for business and governmental entities to extend benefits to the live-in partners of employees. This shows the extent to which our culture is driven not by moral considerations but by economic considerations. Arguing that morality is more important than budget considerations can be a tough sell in today's world.

Reservations Concerning Marriage

Given the high divorce rate, the casual mockery of marriage in our society, and the incredible number of people who have emerged from divorced homes, it's little wonder that many have reservations about the wisdom of getting married. Therefore, many postpone marriage, seeking that elusive certainty that their marriages will work out, and on a superficial level, try-it-before-you-buy-it seems to make sense. Such attitudes may be even more intense among those who've experienced a failed marriage. One cynical person reflected, "When people get married, they're making a contract with their future divorce lawyer."[10] Thus, couples who cohabit are often those who feel very unsure about marriage.

Other fears may also be present. Some cohabitants fear that marriage will have a negative effect on their relationship. Some, influenced by feminism and other modern ideologies, may fear falling into traditional roles, a circumstance they perceive as undesirable. Jenkins illustrates this latter motive by printing a "letter to mother," which lays out a daughter's reasoning for her choice of a cohabiting lifestyle:

> I feel very sure now that John is the best person for me to share my life with. . . . [W]e have come to believe that there are means more conducive to growing a stable relationship than that of marriage. Certainly the examples of failing marriages prevalent in our society today . . . have a negative impact on any goals of marriage for us. . . . So John and I propose to live together for a year to give us time to work out our domestic roles and get a better idea of each other's life goals to be further sure that they can be shared and/or coexist. . . . We each have had several close relationships and do not feel now as much the need for the security of marriage to have one. . . . For people to grow they must be part of an open system and not one that becomes locked in, which is more likely to happen in marriage. In time we hope our relationship will grow sufficiently strong to be able to include the external bond of marriage in a long-term commitment that would include having children.[11]

This letter reflects the classic philosophy that marriage is bondage and cohabitation is bliss. The obvious point it presents is that many people have a great fear of matrimony and look to cohabitation as a way to ensure an eventual successful marriage. Even when these people are shown unmistakable evidence that, should they ever marry, their having cohabited will increase the likelihood of divorce, they still may have trouble trusting marriage. As one young man put it, having just moved in with his girlfriend, "I've been dating the same girl for three years, and it just seemed the natural progression for our relationship— the next step to take. You see so many get divorced that you want to try things out."[12] In order to help such people, someone must show them why marriage is the better choice and how better to prepare.

Conclusion

When people enter cohabiting relationships they may not be clear about their reasons for doing so or aware of all the influences upon them. And later, if they decide to get married, they may not know exactly why they're doing that either. They just may feel that the time is right. Yet they carry into the marriage the same attitudes that led them to cohabit. Can this be good? I've heard cohabiting couples talk about their plans to marry, expressing comments like, "It's just time to settle down"; "We have a child now"; "I'm thirty now, it's about time"; "We'd like to have kids." But these reasons do not form a sufficient foundation for the lifelong commitment of marriage and, in fact, can seriously undermine the potential success of a future marriage.

As has been seen, many explanations and reasons can be presented for the rise in cohabitation. One writer cited a list of these reasons: permissive sexual morals, greater tolerance for alternative lifestyles, disenchantment with traditional dating and marriage, the feminist movement, personal independence and autonomy, narcissism or "me-ism," and desire to avoid the commitment and finality of marriage.[13] With these mind-sets, it's highly likely that any couple who prepares to marry after having cohabited is not as ready or as prepared for the commitment of marriage as they might think. Their views may damage their ability to avoid the one thing they dread the most: the failure of their relationship.

In their hearts, then, they may very much fear matrimony. They fear that marriage will ruin a good relationship. They fear that marriage will end in the disaster of divorce. They fear that marriage demands a higher level of commitment than they can give. They fear that marriage will have economic costs that they're unable or unwilling to pay. Women may have different fears than men, further complicating the unraveling of a couple's resistance to marriage.

Addressing these fears and correcting them is the task of those who seek to minister to cohabiting couples. God has said in His Word that

He "has not given us a spirit of fear, but of power and of love and of a sound mind" (2 Tim. 1:7). The fears deep in the hearts of many cohabiting partners do not come from God, but many couples today are under the influence of values that do not reflect God's wisdom on life. Chances are they've not, in fact, often attended church in recent times. But the knowledge of God and His Word can cast out fears. Thus, such fears can be alleviated, but doing so will take much counsel and teaching. Much of that counsel can be found in the latter parts of this book. First, though, is the need for a more detailed examination of the negative consequences of the cohabiting lifestyle.

Chapter 4

The Consequences of Cohabiting

The Conventional Wisdom

I teach a public speaking class every semester at one of the colleges in our town. The students are mostly freshmen and sophomores, so I get to preside as they practice elementary research and then organize their thoughts for an oral presentation. On some of the assigned speeches, they're given some choice as to subject matter, so occasionally I hear a speech on cohabitation. I've heard presentations both pro and con. On one occasion a female student I'll call Beth gave a speech against cohabitation. Beth's sister experienced a negative "live-in" relationship, so Beth did some homework and found some of the newer research that argues against the wisdom of cohabiting. When she finished, the class had some discussion about the subject.

During the discussion one young man piped up, full of confidence that he could end the discussion once and for all. He said with a smile, "Of course cohabitation is a good idea. Don't you try on a pair of shoes before you buy them?" His brief statement, indeed, silenced the arguments on the other side. Most young students today are steeped in our society's ethic of tolerance, and many are loathe to sharply disagree with one another, believing that everyone is entitled to his or her opinion and every opinion ought to be treated as having validity for the person who holds it.

I don't share this belief. I felt I had to step in. This young man had no way of knowing, of course, that I'd spent several years researching cohabitation with the express intention of challenging the validity of the very analogy he'd made. After I concluded my rebuttal—several minutes later—I think he realized that his little statement wasn't at all the end of the argument.

What, though, is wrong with his argument? If I've heard it once I've heard it a zillion times. One fellow put it like this online in a chat room conversation: "I have married and cohabited, and I noticed that the difference was about $9,990. The divorce cost me $10,000 and telling a girlfriend to get out of my house was about $10. I like option B better. Do you buy a car without test-driving it?"

There are a couple of key problems with this argument. First is the element of time. What car dealer or shoe store do you know that will let someone try out a car or a pair of shoes for a year or eighteen months or longer? Actually, trying on shoes or trying out a car is very casual and is more analogous to dating than cohabitation. Next we have to realize we are dealing with human beings, not inanimate objects.

Do we really want to compare shoes and cars to human beings? If I try on a nice pair of basketball shoes but decide they're not the right fit, do the shoes go back to the box devastated? Do they need counseling before they can trust themselves to another set of feet? Do the smaller (baby) shoes get their hearts broken when I abandon the larger (mother) shoe? Do the shoes feel violated on the deepest level of intimacy when I say I don't want them? When I test-drive a car and decide not to buy it, does the car feel rejected? Does it carry baggage into the next test-driving experience? Are its chances to be a good family car damaged because I didn't buy it?

Test-driving a relationship is only good *if you are the driver.* If you're the girlfriend who gets sent out of the house, it isn't good at all. This analogy shows, in fact, that those who use it and live by it are operating from a posture of unprincipled selfishness that is utterly incompatible with successful and equitable relationships. Do we really want to treat people whom we say we love (or loved at one time) like a car that can be rejected and returned to the lot, like a pair of shoes that can be stuffed back into a box and forgotten? When we cohabit, we're reserving the right to do just that. And the person with whom we cohabit has the same right throughout the entire relationship. This is the cold, hard bottom line.

The "try-it-before-you-buy-it" argument, then, is hardly the best one to use when defending cohabitation. Yet this viewpoint, which for many years represented the conventional wisdom, prevails to some extent into our times. Its strength is waning, which is good, but it needs to be destroyed with no hope of resurrection. How, though, did the argument for cohabitation as a "test-drive for marriage" become so ingrained?

The Birth of the Conventional Wisdom

The essence of the conventional wisdom is that cohabitation is a positive way to prepare for later marriage. It was stated this way by some researchers as recently as 1992: "Many Americans adjusted to the increasing fragility of marriage by opting for nonmarital cohabiting unions. . . . By spending time in these unions, young couples would have better chances of evaluating their relationships, and the less propitious cohabiting unions could be terminated without marriage and the problems of divorce. . . . Because the less propitious cohabiting unions would be terminated and the more positive would be strengthened by the experience of cohabitation, the quality of marriages would be enhanced and the likelihood of divorce reduced."[1]

It's tempting to admit that there's a certain attractive, commonsense appeal to this point of view. It was, in fact, swallowed whole by

American popular culture and is now dying a hard death. What we've learned is that those who cohabit prior to marriage are far more likely than those who do not cohabit to experience later marital disruption, along with a host of other unpleasant realities. Such has been demonstrated time and again. That the conventional wisdom persisted for so long gives proof to the adage, "If you tell a lie long enough, often enough, people start to believe it."

Many of the early proponents of the conventional wisdom were biased in their early assessment of cohabitation. The early studies, which emerged in the 1970s, were not very large and the researchers tended to find only what they wanted to find. And so cohabiters were praised, and cohabitation was greeted as a promising and positive development. Consider this assessment from an early cohabitation researcher:

> Cohabiting women, relative to noncohabiting women, seem to possess a high level of aesthetic appreciation, liberalism, androgyny, and intelligence. These women may have more things going for them if cohabitation or a subsequent marriage does not work out— they have the experience, frame of mind, and orientation to be able to cope in a society with more equitable roles, while women who enter marriage with more traditional notions, expectations, and a high level of dependency may not be so capable. . . . Cohabitors seem to see themselves as more competent, independent, and self-reliant than noncohabitors, and as such may not be as dependent on their relationships for support, contact, and intimacy.[2]

The limited work in the research hardly justified such glowing conclusions. Other exaggerated claims were made about cohabitation in various early studies—for instance, that cohabiting partners had great sex lives, no guilt, and wonderful relationships!

Moreover, in the early days of cohabitation research, glowing predications about the future of the new lifestyle were common. It was believed that living together before marriage would be found as the most effective way to prepare for marriage and that the divorce rate for couples who cohabited would be much lower than for those who entered marriage the more traditional way. But in many cases these early conclusions were highly speculative, almost wishful statements. They were not based in hard research.

But this is how the conventional wisdom was born—a product of mythology. It never was true. But it took hold, not only among researchers, but in the popular media, the popular culture, and in minds of average people, upon whom the falsehoods no doubt wreaked much havoc. When some studies in the 1980s returned information that contradicted the earlier assertions, researchers expressed surprise and marshaled a number of rationalizations to explain away what they were finding. Nonetheless, researchers consistently found that couples who had not cohabited prior to marriage were much more satisfied in their marriages than those who had cohabited.

One researcher, in fact, put his finger on the truth as early as 1981.[3] After discovering that the conventional wisdom was not generally true concerning the eighty-four couples he studied in British Columbia, Watson postulated that cohabiters tended to view marriage negatively because it involved the assumption of new responsibilities that contrasted with their former freedoms. Those who, on the other hand, married through the traditional route didn't feel constrained by marriage, but liberated into a new and exciting dimension of their relationship.

An old hymn rejoices, "Hallelujah, I have found it!" I feel like shouting these words as I type this section, because the point made by Watson more than twenty years ago goes to the heart of the whole discussion on cohabitation. Why does the traditional path of dating and courtship provide a better route to marriage than does cohabitation? Consider that a person in a cohabiting relationship has everything marriage has to offer (including, chiefly, sex) but very few of the responsibilities. So cohabiting persons who enter marriage tend to feel trapped. They assume huge new responsibilities but get nothing that they didn't already have. On the other hand, couples entering marriage through dating and courtship, particularly those who maintain their sexual purity, at long last get to enjoy the full depth of the relationship they've long anticipated. The responsibilities of marriage seem light in comparison to the new privileges. Cohabitation, then, becomes a form of bondage—a sort of catch-22; fear of being trapped in marriage keeps couples trapped in short-term relationships. Couples who do not cohabit prior to marriage, however, consistently report, as a class, greater marital satisfaction than those who do cohabit prior to marriage.

These scenarios are not, of course, absolute. Many couples who enter marriage via the traditional route end up divorced, and couples who've cohabited prior to marriage go on to have happy marriages. Statistics do not doom anyone. The next chapter presents statistical evidence compiled by researchers on the risks associated with cohabiting relationships, and readers will be able to judge for themselves.

This book is not written with a spirit of condemnation but rather with a broken heart, with great sorrow, for those who have taken the road of falsehood and paid the price for it. This book, too, offers hope that the death of the conventional wisdom will help many couples do things the better way.

The Death of the Conventional Wisdom

Even into the 1990s some researchers continued to hope—despite mounting evidence to the contrary—for the success suggested by the conventional wisdom. One pair of researchers wrote in 1990,

> By cohabiting individuals are able to rehearse marital roles, strengthening the future marital bond. Strengthening may occur by developing a mutually satisfactory division of household and market labor, as well as enhancing sexual and interpersonal compatibility. At the same time, if appropriate and satisfactory role relationships cannot be developed, the partners are able to end the relationship before

becoming subject to the additional constraints of the legal system. Following the logic of this position, one would hypothesize that cohabitation should lead to more stable marriages.[4]

The authors adopted this viewpoint even while admitting that the evidence seemed to be stacked against it. Again and again in the 1980s and 1990s, more and more researchers were forced to conclude that the cherished theory they sought to defend was "not supported by the data."[5]

Today it's difficult for anyone to hold out the conventional wisdom as possessing any truth. Heavyweight social commentator Andrew Greeley states, "There is no support for the folk wisdom that premarital sex of one variety or another is a preparation for marital happiness."[6] Some still attempt to explain the higher divorce rate and poorer marital experience of those who cohabit prior to marriage without admitting that something inherent in the cohabiting experience causes the failures. In reality, however, cohabitation produces less commitment to, and less enjoyment of, marriage.

Such should not surprise us. As Linda Waite says, "Marriage forms a new union. Cohabiting is more like roommates with sex."[7] The arguments to the contrary, though, will likely persist. Cherished, sacred cows die hard. Some researchers today want to remove any moral judgments on cohabitation, arguing that it's just another way of forming family ties. And if the unions break up more often and experience more trouble than do traditional marriages, that's merely the result of people having the freedom to make their own choices. This new argument seems a cruel one, indeed, and likely is offered by those who've never ministered to people trying to recover from the wounds of a failed relationship.

It would be an answer to prayer if the conventional wisdom's death were reported as widely, as enthusiastically, and as long as its birth. Such is not yet the case. George Barna reported in 1993 that 60 percent of Americans believed that the best way to establish a successful marital relationship was to cohabit prior to marriage.[8] Heidi Kauffman reports that the Civil Liberties Union of Harvard University conducted a survey in which 91 percent of undergraduates were in favor of coed rooming at the university.[9] There's no doubt that the conventional wisdom is deeply embedded in modern popular culture, and many are making choices consistent with it. It can be hoped, however, that people will begin to see things differently. Perhaps the popular media will do the right thing in their reporting and portray the truth about cohabitation in a more honest and correct fashion.

One young person in *Parade* gave me some hope. In a small opinion survey on the merits of cohabitation, she said, "If love is blind, sex is the blindfold. . . . Someone said that you need to live together to see if a person will satisfy you sexually. If a person is kind, patient, loving, respectful, thoughtful, clean, and not egotistical, those very nonsexual things will carry over into the bed. Nature will do the rest."[10] Of course it will. It always has. *Reader's Digest* has also printed a moving plea for traditional courtship, coming from a mother brokenhearted over her daughter's decision to cohabit.[11] The arguments presented were surprisingly strong and clear, citing some of the newer research. They read like nails in the coffin of the conventional wisdom and bear repeating here:

1. There's a good chance that a couple living together will never tie the knot.
2. If live-in couples do marry, they run a higher risk of divorce.
3. Breaking up can hurt as much as divorce.
4. Even if cohabiting couples do marry, such couples are often less happy.
5. Cohabiters have all of the problems of marriage with none of the rewards.

This must become the new conventional wisdom. Whether or not it does, and the effect it has upon our culture, remains to be seen. But it's clear that the conventional wisdom is, indeed, dead. The obituary has not yet been printed everywhere, but a death has occurred.

This chapter began with an analogy about cohabitation: "You try on a shoe before you buy it, don't you?" Perhaps it's fitting to end with another analogy, but one that more effectively captures the emptiness and danger of the cohabiting lifestyle. It comes from Jennifer Roback Morse, who readily admits that she and her husband cohabited prior to marriage, only to find out, once married, how much they had to unlearn from their days of cohabiting.[12] She argues that there's a better analogy of cohabitation than the shoe or car scenario:

> Suppose I ask you to give me a blank check, signed and ready to cash. All I have to do is fill in the amount. Most people would be unlikely to do this. You would be likely to do it, if you snuck out and drained the money out of your account before you gave me the check. Or, you could give me the check and just be scared about what I might do. Think about it: What do you have in your checking account that is more valuable than what you give a sexual partner? When people live together and have sex together, without marriage, they put themselves in a position that is similar to the person being asked to give a blank check. They either hold back on their partner by not giving the full self in the sexual act and in their shared lives together. Or they feel scared a lot of the time, wondering whether their partner will somehow take advantage of their vulnerability. No one can simulate self-giving. Half a commitment is no commitment. Cohabiting couples are likely to have one foot out the door throughout the relationship. The members of a cohabiting couple practice holding back on one another. They rehearse not trusting. The social scientists that gather the data do not have a way to measure this kind of dynamic inside the relationship.

Indeed they don't.

Chapter 5

The Consequences of Cohabiting

The Hard Realities

The church at which I'm one of the pastors has a modern, attractive facility. Consequently, we receive many requests for weddings, even from those who don't attend our church. Brides-to-be have even come to the worship center and taken a video of it for a comparative video file in order to choose just the right place to be married! I suppose they want to make sure all the colors are coordinated or something. Most pastors, however, are more encouraged by a couple who's excited and focused upon the marriage rather than upon the details of the wedding. The focus of the couple almost always reveals some things about the couple and their relationship.

For various other reasons, to be addressed in a later chapter, we're reluctant to perform weddings for those who don't attend our church, but I've met with many couples who are interested in getting married. Among the many questions I ask them in an initial interview is one about living together prior to marriage: "Are you now, have you in the past, or do you plan to live together prior to your wedding in any way, shape, or form?" I ask the question this way because I've found that couples are tempted to answer questions about living together in a way that's less than the truth, the whole truth, and nothing but the truth. They might say, for example, "No, we're not living together," but then they'll move in together later on, prior to the wedding. Or they'll say, "No, we're not living together," but they've cohabited in the past for a significant period of time. Or they may say, "No, we're not living together," but they do spend several nights a week together. So I've found that it's important to cover all the bases with my question.

Why do I ask such a question? Am I nosy? Do I like to rummage around in other people's business? No, I ask out of concern for the couple. If I'm going to counsel with them prior to marriage and do my best to prepare them for a successful marriage, I need to know if they've ever lived together, for how long, and why they did it. That information is one of a number of things I need to know about them. And I ask this specific question because I know the realities that are likely to ensue in a relationship if a couple has cohabited prior to marriage. And I ask because I care for the couple; I'm committed to helping them establish a proper foundation for their marriage. This chapter is about the negative realities of cohabitation. The last chapter touched upon some of them in general terms; this chapter outlines them with greater clarity, making a thorough survey of the negative realities of cohabitation.

Choosing the Right Partner

One of the arguments long made by proponents of the cohabiting lifestyle is that cohabitation will have a positive effect on what is called "partner choice," that is, making a wise decision about who we spend our lives with. The theory is that cohabitation will provide an opportunity for a couple to learn whether or not they are compatible for a later marriage. Those who find out they are compatible will go on to have a strong marriage; those who find out they are not compatible will dissolve their relationship before they commit themselves to marriage. Cohabitation, therefore—so the argument goes—gives a superior opportunity to determine whether one's live-in companion will be a good partner for life. Those who enter marriage through traditional courtship do not have this kind of opportunity. It was suggested for years by many researchers that because of this "partner choice" opportunity, couples who had cohabited before marriage would make a better choice of partner and be much less likely to divorce after marriage.

In truth, though, cohabiting couples tend to do quite poorly when it comes to partner selection. First, many cohabiting relationships do not lead to marriage. One study suggests that in more recent years only 50 percent to 60 percent of first time cohabiters end up marrying the person they live with.[1] When the number of these cohabiting couples who break up were added to the number who cohabited, married, and subsequently divorced, as many as 80 percent of couples who cohabit will end their relationship at some point![2] This is an important statistic, not to be lightly passed over. It's apparent that in most cohabiting relationships, a poor partner choice is made. Think, then, of all the turmoil, disappointment, and heartache that go along with all this breaking up and divorce.

Further, one study in Canada found that most cohabiting relationships do not endure for long periods. Fewer than half, in fact, survive for just three years.[3] Another study indicated that 40 percent of cohabiting unions do not continue for even a year; only one-third survive for two years; for couples who remain in a cohabiting relationship without marrying, only between 25 percent and 33 percent survive for five years. And the survival rate for ten years is only between 12 percent and 15 percent.[4] In contrast to all of this, nineteen out of twenty first marriages survive for two years,[5] and 90 percent survive to ten years.[6] The clear conclusion is that only in a modest number of cases do the partners chosen for a cohabiting relationship prove to be long-term companions. If, then, cohabitation does not lead to marriage, about 90 percent of these relationships are doomed to failure. And even if the couples marry, they will more than likely divorce; those cohabiting unions that end in marriage are "almost twice as likely to dissolve within ten years."[7]

If, then, a person enters a cohabiting relationship or is in a cohabiting relationship, statistically speaking, that person has most likely *not* chosen a companion with whom he or she will spend the rest of their lives. If, on the other hand, that same person were instead to date and court in the traditional way, statistically speaking, he or she will choose a partner who will be far more likely to become a lifelong companion. Marriage carries no guarantees, of course, but it's foolish to become blind to the realities of the above statistics. So if we as pastors and advisors are counseling with a person who's cohabiting, we must be aware that the person or couple in front of us is almost surely headed for a breakup at some point or another. On a personal level, I certainly feel a serious obligation to talk with cohabiting couples about these disturbing statistics.

Cohabiting couples, then, tend not to choose partners they end up spending their lives with, and in addition their relationships tend to be relatively brief. And even when the cohabiting relationship leads to marriage, the marriages are far more likely to be short lived. Kristin and Matt met each other, moved in together, and married, all in a relatively short period of time. She was a successful professional woman; he was a bit of a local celebrity. In their early thirties, they were both well paid and very attractive in the superficial sense. They came to me for counseling in their first year of marriage with complaints that things weren't working out. As I counseled with them, it became apparent to me that they'd fallen in love with each other's image and really didn't know each other. They both had significant problems in terms of being a good spouse. He was vain, selfish, immature, and temperamental; she was moody, cold, and controlling. They both had a lot of growing up to do, but neither of them realized any of this when they first met each other and moved in together. Their relationship was intimate before either of them really had a clue who the other person was. I cringed when I thought what it must have been like to be in their home. They ended up divorcing, still not quite comprehending what had happened. Because they moved to other parts of the country, I don't know what became of either of them, but given the lack of insight they possessed concerning their relationship, I feared greatly for any subsequent relationships either of them would enter, and even warned them.

Clearly, cohabitation is not helping people make wise choices. The old Puritans used to counsel young people not to marry because they were in "love." They feared that the ardor of youthful love could cloud good judgment. Instead, they counseled that young people should marry *in order to love,* and concentrate on choosing a potential mate who would make a good and godly companion for life. The casual way that couples enter cohabiting relationships works against this kind of wise choosing, and a lot of breaking up occurs because of it. Anyone who's been in a cohabiting relationship may need thorough help in thinking through whether or not they've made a good choice and what kind of person makes a good, long-term companion.

Children

The common image of cohabiting couples as young, unattached college or career types is not entirely valid. In 40 percent of all cohabiting unions children are present. The number rises to 50 percent for cohabitants who've had previous marriages. Nor are the children babies and toddlers. One-fourth of all cohabiting households have children ten or older.[8] Thus, many cohabitants are parents and "step-parents." But is this a good idea for the children?

There has not been all that much research done on the direct impact of cohabitation on children, but there are some points that should be made. Notice this distressing report: . . . 10 percent of children born between 1960 and 1968 were born outside of marriage and before age 16, another 19 percent experienced the dissolution of their parents' marriage. When parental death and other causes of family disruption are also considered, 36 percent of the children (in this group) had been separated from at least one parent before they reached age 16. . . . In all 27 percent of nonmarital births between 1970 and 1984 were to cohabiting couples. . . . About two-thirds of cohabiting couples who had children during the 1970s eventually married; however before these children reach age 16, *56 percent of them are likely to experience the disruption of their parents' marriage.* (emphasis added)[9]

This information, coupled with the high rate of cohabitation among those who have been previously married (about two-thirds of second marriages are preceded by cohabitation), indicates that the family situation in which many children find themselves is highly transitional. Having a child together does not necessarily mean that a given cohabiting couple will marry and go on to form a stable union for their child or children. The relationships remain very volatile. Consider some further research findings:

. . . 56% of children born to cohabiting couples who later marry will experience the disruption of their parents' marriage, compared with about 31% of children born to married parents. When this proportion is combined with the one-third whose cohabiting parents break up without marrying, *it appears that about three-quarters of children of cohabiting couples will spend some time in a single parent home.* . . . *relatively few children of cohabiting couples will reach age 16 in an intact family.* (emphasis added)[10]

These statistics are deeply troubling, and they represent far more than numbers; they represent children who need and deserve an intact home. I've often found it difficult to get people in a troubled marriage to think about the welfare of their children. How much more difficult, then, to get cohabiters to think of the welfare of their children, since they've made individualistic choices to begin with. Imagine the lives of the children whose homes are unstable. Your parents are unmarried and merely live together. Or your married parents have split up and one or both are remarried to new spouses, or are cohabiting with someone. Then, perhaps, one or both parents' relationships dissolve and others ensue. Would you want that kind of life? Can this, in most instances, be a good thing for a child?

In addition, one study found that children of unmarried cohabiting biological parents are twenty times more likely to be abused than the children of married parents. When a mother lives with a boyfriend who is not the biological father, the children are thirty-three times more likely to be abused. Cohabitation is a disaster for children.[11]

Grown-ups must see that their decision making must include the welfare of their children. It's well documented that multiple family transitions represent a powerful source of stress and maladjustment on the part of children. Children who do not grow up in stable, intact families simply do not receive the same investment of parental care as those who do. I've explained to many people, many times: it's not the responsibility of children to sacrifice for their parents; it's the responsibility of parents to sacrifice for their children. Parents have an obligation to provide a stable home for their children. That our culture accepts such easy cohabitation and lack of marital commitment has clearly led to a decline in the stability of the homes in which our children are reared. Another unpleasant reality of the cohabiting lifestyle is that behind the statistics cited above are thousands and perhaps millions of children harmed by their parents' willingness to embrace cohabitation.

Legal Rights

Most states have decriminalized cohabitation but, strictly speaking, it's still illegal in a few states. The laws, however, are obviously not enforced. Laws vary from state to state, of course, but by not marrying, couples do put themselves at a legal disadvantage. Apart from explicit legal agreements, cohabiting couples may risk their custody rights to children from a previous marriage or lose support payments from a previous spouse. Cohabiters will not be able to authorize emergency medical treatment for their partners, and most employers still do not grant spousal type benefits to cohabiting partners.

When a cohabiting couple breaks up, most courts, in the absence of a specific statute, grant settlements on the basis of the old concept of "equity" or whatever seems fair in regard to property or financial claims. Most lawyers advise cohabiting couples not to make any promises—oral or written—to each other, counseling that each should maintain separate incomes and bank accounts, and hold separate property. Separate, separate, separate. This doesn't seem the best word upon which to build a relationship, does it?

One Web site, discussing matters from a legal standpoint, suggests several things a cohabiting partner should never do:

1. Never contribute money to the acquisition of a major asset (like a house or a car) that is held solely in the name of your partner.
2. Never become financially dependent upon your partner to the point that a breakup would leave you financially devastated. In other words, keep your own job.
3. Never let your partner have any doubt about your intentions. If, for example, you receive a financial gift from your partner or you loan your partner some money, get a signed agreement.
4. Never put money in a joint account or hold title to assets in joint names. Avoid all joint ownership.[12]

The site advises that if a couple avoids these "nevers" they will likely avoid "a lot of heartache." That the admonitions presume the volatility of cohabiting relationships is very revealing. But then again, aren't lawyers paid to be realists? There are, after all, few incentives for these relationships to remain intact and almost no legal incentives to do so. Still, breaking up isn't all that simple. The complications that emerge when a cohabiting couple dissolves their union can be complex and troubling, involving issues of money, division of property, spousal support or "palimony," and child custody. Those cohabiting couples who think they'll emerge from a broken relationship without any of these entanglements should think again.

Nor are the U.S. Congress and state legislatures in a hurry to enact legal protections for cohabiting partners. For reasons that should be obvious, legislative bodies are reluctant to tamper with well-settled marriage laws. Ruth Deech has pointed to the philosophical obstacle that resists changing the legalities governing marriage and cohabitation. She put it bluntly but stated it as many see it, saying that

> . . . if cohabitants are dissatisfied with their legal position . . . the question must be asked, "Why don't they marry?" Moreover, many cohabitants do not marry precisely because they wish to retain certain perceived benefits that would be lost if they married. People can choose cohabitation today with little social stigma. It appears to be the prevailing wisdom that they be permitted to choose between the various arrangements that are available. There is little groundswell for changing the legal implications.[13]

It seems unlikely, then, that the legal status of cohabitation will ever be blanketed with the legal protections of marriage. Thus, the lack of legal status for cohabiting couples provides few incentives to stay together, and can be seen as almost expecting and encouraging the dissolution of relationships. Such lack of legal standing is yet another of the negative consequence for deciding to enter into cohabitation.

Violence

Another negative reality of a cohabiting relationship is the increased potential for violence in these relationships compared with marriage and traditional dating. Statistics indicate that cohabiting couples have a significantly higher rate of "minor" episodes of violence such as pushing, slapping, shoving, grabbing, or throwing an object, as well as for more severe acts of violence such as biting, kicking, punching, hitting with an object, beatings, or threatening to use a gun or a knife.[14]

Although most cohabiting relationships do not involve violence of any kind, cohabitation does seem to create a more fertile ground for violence between couples. Why? Scholars and researchers have suggested some reasons:

1. Cohabiting couples are more isolated from a network of peers and family; the extreme individualism of the cohabitation philosophy diminishes to some extent the involvement of others who would provide a check on violence, as they do in dating and marital relationships.
2. The question of control and independence may be more volatile in cohabiting relationships, with more frequent disputing over rights, duties, and obligations. It is noteworthy that cohabiting couples seek out periods of separation and counseling more frequently than do married couples.
3. The heavy investment in the relationship required by the live-in situation of cohabiting couples is surely weighty enough to spawn many kinds of conflict, yet there are fewer of the features of marriage that would restrain violence, including the long-term commitment to the relationship.[15]

In short, it may be that cohabiters have a more difficult time negotiating which elements in their relationship should be a matter of independence and which should be a matter of togetherness. Regardless of the motive, however, episodes of humiliating and harmful violence are more frequent in cohabiting relationships, and are another negative reality. Such indicates that cohabiters find it much harder to have a healthy relationship.

Religion

A relationship is well established between decreased religious involvement and cohabitation. Couples who cohabit tend to be less religious in general, and those couples who are religious, once they enter a cohabiting relationship, tend to avoid religious involvement. On the other hand, couples who get married tend to increase their religious involvement. This circumstance is not surprising but it is distressing, particularly for those of us who approach matters from a biblical and Christian viewpoint. At the very point when people most need support, instruction, and moral guidance (when they settle down with a partner), they opt out of the church. A detachment from moral and religious support, then, is another negative consequence of cohabitation.

Some modern thinkers want the church to modify its thinking on marriage and morality to accommodate cohabitants. Such is not likely to happen. Most Christians believe that marriage descends from God and that cohabitation is a violation of His will; that is, it is sinful. It's tempting for pastors, churches, and Christians to see themselves at odds with cohabiters because cohabiters are, after all, at odds with God. Cohabiters, no doubt sensing or realizing this conflict, fear rejection by the church. But a cohabiting couple desperately needs the counsel of the church.

It is thus important for pastors to remain open to meeting with cohabiting couples. We should look for those opportunities to share without apology what God's plan is for marriage, sex, and family. For some cohabiters, that plan may not be at all what they want to hear, but for all, it will be what they need to hear. And God may just use it to change the direction of some lives.

Sometimes when a cohabiting couple begins to think about marriage they'll also begin to think about returning to the church, and perhaps not just for a wedding event. Pastors and churches must be ready for this eventuality with a message and a plan. A later chapter in this book offers specific suggestions on how to do so. The church may tend to view cohabitation as a threat to marriage, but remember that many cohabiting couples do desire to be married at some point. It would be well, then, to give these couples the benefit of the doubt and minister to them in a productive way.

The best scenario, of course, is to instruct young people in the sanctity of marriage, spelling out the negative realities of the cohabiting lifestyle long before they fall into it. It nonetheless remains a sad reality that cohabiting couples take a sojourn from the church at precisely the time they need it the most. And cohabiting relationships are bearing the unhealthy fruit of too little guidance, accountability, and instruction. Over the course of my years of pastoral work, I've performed dozens of weddings, counseling with the couples as carefully and thoroughly as I know how. The vast majority are still together and seem to be enjoying reasonably healthy marriages. Thus, we must be doing something right in the church. And cohabiting couples must be doing something wrong. Cohabiting couples need the church and they need the voice of God.

Men Versus Women

As pointed out earlier, men and women tend to go into a cohabiting relationship with different attitudes and expectations. The point is not whether a cohabiting couple has a traditional or more egalitarian approach to gender roles (actually both kinds of relationships exist among cohabiters); the point is that the man and the woman often have different motives for moving in together. One large study found that men clearly tend to have a lower commitment to their partner and to the relationship than do women.[16]

Women are much more likely to be attracted to a cohabiting relationship because they believe it will more likely ensure the stability of the relationship. They tend to view cohabitation, in fact, as a step toward a long-term relationship that may lead to marriage. Men tend to have a more practical view of cohabitation. One man, for example, commented on the apparent divergence of views: "When I first asked her [to move in with me] she looked at me like I was asking a momentous thing. And I scratched my head because it wasn't momentous to me. . . . She said, 'You don't attach much importance to this?' 'No,' [I said], 'It's just that you can come and stay with me, that's all.'"[17] Men are more likely to desire a cohabiting relationship for reasons other than the expectation of marriage. And they may also be less likely to adopt an ethic of sexual faithfulness in the relationship.[18] Men, too, are more likely than women to become "serial" cohabiters, having several subsequent cohabiting relationships.

It appears, then, that it's common for men and women who are in a cohabiting relationship to enter cohabitation with two different "blueprints" for the future. It is thus not surprising that many of these relationships end badly, particularly for the woman. Women who live with men more readily expect that at some point they will marry the men with whom they're living. But studies show that men move much slower and much less readily to marriage. It's been suggested, in fact, that men move toward marriage at the pace of a "wounded sloth."[19] And when they do agree to marry, they are more likely to be less committed to it than are women. Men do fear divorce more and are more likely to believe that living together is simply easier and less complicated. Women, who tend to display a greater willingness to sacrifice for others, tend to be the ones who get hurt.[20] Greeley—in his study of cohabitation, marriage, and premarital sex—made a bleak observation: "With some exceptions, men are the winners and with some exceptions women are the losers. So what else is new?"[21] Those who counsel with cohabiting couples or with those thinking about cohabitation ought to point out these facts to women. In the church, pastors should be eager to share these kinds of dynamics, especially with young people, with the hope that they avoid the obvious pitfalls as they seek a marriage partner.

In contrast to the above disparity in perception, dating, courting and marrying in the traditional way allows for a clearer meeting of the minds between men and women. A greater likelihood occurs that both the man and the woman are coming to the marriage with the same understanding of the commitment involved, particularly when solid premarital counseling is part of the equation. Cohabiting unions, on the other hand, can be entered with little foresight or deep thinking. Little wonder, then, that marriages are more stable when not preceded by cohabitation and far more stable than cohabiting relationships.

Marital Satisfaction

Marital satisfaction for those who cohabit and then go on to wed tends to be lower from the very earliest stages of the marital union. Higher levels of communication problems occur, as well as disagreements, instability, and, of course, subsequent divorce. Couples who cohabit are, in fact, more likely to be unhappy in marriage and more likely to think about divorce.[22] And, in an interesting finding, at least one study shows that all of the problems are made worse for those who cohabited for longer periods of time.[23]

Barna states that, when compared to couples who did not cohabit, those who did were characterized by all of the following attributes:

1. They show lower levels of overall marital satisfaction.
2. They have a lower overall commitment to marriage as an institution.
3. They are less likely to see their spouse as their best friend.
4. They are less likely to believe that their spouse respects them.
5. They have a greater fear of divorce.
6. They are more restless about their marriage and outside relationships.[24]

Why, though, do postcohabitation marriages evince these attributes? One study, which analyzed the attitudes of couples, placed blame on the individualistic attitudes of those who previously cohabited.[25] Cohabiters know that reasonable alternatives to marriage exist; before marriage they experienced a scenario in which they kept their singleness but also had a full domestic and sexual relationship. However the dissatisfaction is explained, the research clearly demonstrates that couples who go on to marry after cohabiting are less likely to find the happiness they desire. This is yet another ugly reality of the cohabiting lifestyle.

Marital Breakups

Several theories explain why couples who cohabit and go on to marry end up in divorce court at a far higher rate than couples who enter marriage through the traditional route. One idea claims that, for practical purposes, cohabiters begin their domestic relationship much earlier than the wedding day, allowing more time in comparison to other married couples for divisive conflicts to emerge. It's also been suggested that cohabiting couples are simply less committed to marriage than the more traditional couple.

But is there something about the cohabiting relationship itself that has a corrupting effect on a subsequent marriage? There may be. There can no longer be disagreement that the marriages of cohabiters break up at a far higher rate than those who have not cohabited. One comprehensive study cited some thirteen research projects in the 1980s and 1990s that documented this phenomenon is an established fact.[26] Consider the numbers. Unions begun by a cohabiting relationship are almost twice as likely to dissolve within ten years (57%) when compared with all first marriages (30%). The gap is huge in the first two years (cohabiting—29%; married—9%).[27] The rate is even higher for those who have cohabited with someone other than their future spouse or who have been in some fashion a serial cohabiter (multiple cohabitation experiences). More recent studies suggest the figure is rising. A standard figure cited in the popular media today is that couples who cohabit prior to marriage are almost twice as likely to divorce than those who entered marriage the traditional way.

These numbers are, indeed, sobering. And couples, if not increasingly aware of these statistics, seem to anticipate them. In one study, for instance, when married persons were asked to predict the likelihood of a divorce, over 60 percent of the couples who had not cohabited prior to marriage stated the possibility of divorce was very low, while only 38 percent of couples who had previously cohabited said so.[28]

What are the reasons for this disparity of opinion? Let me suggest a few:

1. Individuals who cohabit are less likely to agree with the traditional notions of marriage and family. They have more liberal viewpoints on matters such as divorce and premarital sex, and they may have less respect for the institution of marriage. So they enter marriage with a view that diminishes the importance of marriage and family.
2. Individuals who cohabit may be more resistant to commitment. In cohabitation, they've tried to test out a relationship of commitment by remaining uncommitted. Does that make sense?
3. Individuals who cohabit enter a full sexual relationship, often long before the real issues of the relationship have been sorted out. This early engagement in a sexual relationship may cloud or short-circuit the forethought that is needed for long-term partner choice.
4. Individuals who cohabit prior to marriage may have trouble shedding the individualism that has characterized their lives prior to marriage.
5. The partners who cohabit may be deceived into thinking that marriage will be just like their previous state. But

emotionally, legally, socially, and in other ways, they're surprised to learn it's different. There are more obligations than they may have thought and they respond negatively.

Prior to marriage, a cohabiter may have anxiety that the partner might tire of the relationship and decide to leave. But after marriage, that same person may feel trapped by the commitment of marriage. These feelings of fear and entrapment undermine the marriage. The person still has some residual fear carried over from the cohabiting period, that the partner can just leave; at the same time the person experiences new and unpleasant feelings of greater obligation and commitment. In a sad irony, the one thing cohabiters often fear more than anything else—divorce—is the very thing they fall into at a far higher rate than those who do not cohabit. To cohabiters, this fact should perhaps be the most sobering reality of all.

Conclusion

From this lengthy discussion of the negative realities of cohabitation, it's clear that cohabitation is not a good idea. It leads to less consideration and thought regarding the choice of a partner. It puts children at risk of an unstable and damaging home life. It offers fewer legal protections. There's far greater potential, too, for violence when in a cohabiting relationship. Cohabitation tends to isolate couples from the church and other avenues of instruction and accountability. Women are far more likely to end up being used in the cohabiting lifestyle. Cohabitation also leads to greater unhappiness, disruption, and divorce in subsequent marriages.

As pastors and others engage in discussions with couples in cohabiting relationships or at risk to cohabit, these hard realities should be pointed out. Many years ago, one writer captured the reality of cohabitation with these words: . . . the living together arrangement has very little to support its continuance aside from the affection of two people. Either party is free to withdraw any day. There can be no planning for the future. . . . Neither partner gives any promise of loyalty. No surrounding circle of family and friends can defend their togetherness. Any passing flirtation attractive to either party can terminate the arrangement. Any disagreement may lead to separation. Long-range goals of companionship and the establishment of a home and family fare poorly for a couple who prefer to make no binding commitments to one another.[29]

It's not easy to build a marriage on this foundation. And, even if marriage is not in the picture for a cohabiting couple, how long can such a foundation support a relationship? These unstable elements outlined by the writer above constitute the core of cohabiting arrangements and militate against long-term successful relationships and marriages. The elements constitute, too, the essential negative realities and consequence of cohabitation. It is a further unfortunate reality that many continue to choose this path.

A simple doctrine will be outlined in succeeding chapters, and it can eliminate all the negatives. It's called sexual purity and the covenant of marriage. It involves waiting for God's choice of a life partner and sealing it with a vow and a pledge. What needless harm a person avoids by following this simple doctrine! And how far we have moved away from it in modern America.

Chapter 6

What Does the Bible Say About Cohabitation?

One pastor described his dealings with a cohabiting couple who began attending his church.[1] The occasion arose when he felt he must be truthful with them about how God saw their lifestyle. His "stomach tightened" and his "friendly grin suddenly developed rigor mortis." These symptoms of fear stemmed from a previous occasion when he'd counseled with a cohabiting couple concerning the sinfulness of their lifestyle. The man gave him a "hostile stare" and the woman left the meeting in tears. It did not go well.

People in the cohabiting lifestyle may not always be interested in the correction of God's Word or the admonitions of God's servant. They may not perceive that what they're doing is morally wrong. And if they do realize it's wrong, they may not see it as all *that* wrong.

Pastors, though, need to talk frankly to couples about cohabitation. It would help the discussion if we pastors had a deep and trusted friendship with those we talk to in this way. But this isn't always possible. Despite all the kindness we can muster, such a meeting may not go well. From my research with pastors, I'd say we see more "failures" than successes in these situations, if we define *success* as getting a couple to rectify their lifestyle. Yet are these "failures" really failures? Isn't it the calling of pastors to be faithful to God's Word? If pastors are faithful in speaking the truth in love, how can that be considered a failure, even if the desired outcome is not immediately seen? It's not the calling of pastors to be in step with the times. It's the calling of pastors to call the times to be in step with God.

As a pastor, I perform an initial interview with each couple seeking a wedding. Sometimes I know the couple very well, sometimes not. Through the years, during this interview I have occasionally discovered that the couple is living together. To put people at ease, I pass over this at first until I've completed all the other questions. But I do return to the issue, and I have some standard comments that I make to such couples. These comments are, in fact, typed in the little notebook I use for premarital counseling, and I casually turn to them at some point in the conversation. I don't let on that I'm reading the remarks to the couple, but I do share the substance of what I've written in the notebook. The comments cover such things as the hard realities of the cohabiting lifestyle, what the Bible says about it, as well as what I feel the couple should do (the substance of these remarks appear in appendix B of this book). Sometimes one or both of the partners doesn't like what he or she is hearing, and they react with some surprise and even anger that I would presume to talk with them about their lifestyle. They came in looking for a wedding, after all, not a sermon. Such is the nature of pastoral work in our times.

My aim on such occasions is simply to present the wisdom of the Scriptures on the cohabiting lifestyle. I offer some practical warnings as well as possible solutions to the moral dilemma faced by both the couple and by the pastor as a representative of God's church. Later this book offers specifics of these solutions. This chapter, however, reviews the clear teaching of God's word on cohabitation, for surely we need to understand this teaching as we contemplate counseling with cohabiting couples. Those who believe the Scriptures understand that marriage and morality descend from God, and this is where our moral outlook on cohabitation begins.

It's probably no surprise that the Bible views cohabitation not as an alternative to marriage or an approximation of marriage, but a rejection of it. Such is not a difficult thing to demonstrate, but it's not always easy to share these truths with a cohabiting couple, especially when we have a longing to see them open their hearts to Christ and be welcomed into God's church. It's best, however, for us to share the truth with such couples. Who doesn't enter God's church on the basis of repentance for sins? How can people repent unless they know their sin? So let's prepare ourselves to share without apology God's view of marriage and cohabitation. Many passages could be cited, but two simple yet clear passages of the New Testament place cohabitation squarely in the category of being a clear rejection of God's ordinance of marriage.

First Corinthians 5:1–13

I've visited the ruins of the ancient city of Corinth. It's located near the sea, just south of a little isthmus of land that today has a canal dug through it. On the one side is the Aegean Sea; on the other is the Ionian Sea. It must have been quite a city in its day, connecting east and west, with passing ships often dragged on rollers over the land where the canal is now. Prosperous and worldly, ancient Corinth boasted a large marketplace and numerous temples built to honor pagan gods. But even more than this, the city was known for its immoral ways. To engage in extramarital sex was, in the ancient world, to "corinthianize." Many of the pagan temples had standard rituals that involved sex with prostitutes. The moral climate was thus quite polluted.

The apostle Paul came to Corinth and established a church. It later became a troubled church, although one that Paul loved with great tenderness. First Corinthians 5:1–13 was recorded in the first of two

extant letters Paul subsequently wrote to this church, addressing some
of the problems. One problem that needed particular attention was a
report Paul had received (v. 1) about *porneia,* which was a broad term
in the original Greek for sexual sin. The report was of a severe kind of
sexual sin, one that Paul stated was not even practiced among the
Gentiles (non-Jews) let alone among devout Christians. This was quite
a statement given that the Roman world in general and the Corinthian
people in particular practiced vast sexual license. One ancient commentator captured the sexual ethic of the day: "Mistresses we keep
for the sake of pleasure, concubines for the daily care of the body, but
wives to bear us legitimate children."[2]

The sin in view in this passage was a sexual relationship between a
man who was evidently a professing Christian and a woman who had
been his father's wife. The relationship had three strikes against it
from a biblical point of view. First, it was considered incestuous, a
relationship spoken against by the Old Testament (Lev. 18:8; Deut.
22:30). Second was the matter of a Christian participating in a lifestyle
like this, with a woman who was apparently not a Christian (no re-
buke was given to her). Third, no marital union is explicitly mentioned in the text. This relationship was, in fact, a kind of cohabitation,
what might have been called in that era *concubinage.* Paul expressed
some outrage over this illicit relationship, since it appeared that the
"sinful activity had been going on for some time and was still going
on. It was not a onetime or short-term affair but was continuous and
open . . . living together as man and wife."[3] The Christian assembly
had apparently done nothing to correct the man's behavior.

Note that the apostle Paul, with absolutely no second thoughts or
reservations, named such a relationship *sinful.* And since one of the
parties was a Christian Paul wanted the sinful situation corrected immediately. He seemed to operate from the perspective that there are
two kinds of sexual relationships: marriage—and every other kind.
And every other kind, including cohabitation, is sinful. It displeased
Paul that some of the Christians seemed to treat this sinful behavior as

a matter of Christian liberty, as if Christians had the freedom to alter God's moral commands. Such was not the correct moral evaluation.

The rest of the passage concerns the steps that Paul outlined for the church in order that this brother might correct his lifestyle, get out of the relationship, and return to a holy and moral way of living. He also soundly warned the church about the corrupting influence of this lifestyle if it continued to be tolerated (vv. 6–8). These are sobering words for our own day.

Paul made it clear, then, that such a lifestyle is not acceptable to God. Certainly it is permissible to minister to people who are in such lifestyles (vv. 9–13), but with a view that they be called from their sins to faith in Christ. And once a person is "in Christ" this kind of lifestyle becomes utterly inappropriate since it involves a rejection of God's ordinance of marriage and the sexual ethic He has prescribed for humanity.

It's clear, then, that cohabiting relationships are placed in the category of sexual sin. They are not marriages. They are not trial marriages. They are not quasi marriages. Disguising them under terms like "committed relationships" or "domestic partnerships" doesn't change their status. We should not view them with ambiguity: cohabitation is sexual sin. These unions are unholy unions. Those of us who operate from a biblical perspective have no right to weaken this understanding, whatever the point of view held by the surrounding culture. That cohabitation is sinful must be brought home to us, just as Paul brought it home to the Corinthians.

In the large body of sociological and demographic studies of cohabitation that I've read and examined, very few included moral judgments concerning cohabitation such as the one Paul made in this passage. Cohabitation is called everything from quasi marriage to a new and improved method of human coupling. But such is the wisdom of the world. We've already seen where that wisdom gets us. In this text, the Bible makes a different judgment. Cohabitation is sexual sin, sexual license that falls well short of God's plan for humanity.

John Calvin, writing in the sixteenth century, commented on the situation in this text, calling it "abominable and execrable whoredom."[4] The modern world no doubt finds such language antiquated and laughable, and we may not likely use it ourselves. Still we should, like Calvin, have the courage to call cohabitation sinful, even if people will not accept this evaluation. People have a need to hear what God thinks. His judgment of human behavior is not open to negotiation—and God has spoken about this kind of living. Should we, then, be surprised when we see devastating consequences emerge from the widespread practice of this lifestyle? We are not listening to our Maker.

Nor were Greg and Jeanette. They met in a rural area where Greg was a truck driver who made trips to a small factory where Jeanette worked. They began to date and quickly progressed to a sexual relationship. Before long they were living together. They eventually got married, had some children, and settled down in their life together. Years later, having been invited to church by a friend, they heard me explain, among other things, God's standards for sex and marriage. They eventually became Christians—the Spirit of God bringing salvation to their hearts—and became active in the church. On one occasion Greg shared with me that he and Jeanette, in the depths of their repentance as they came to faith in Christ, admitted to one another that they'd done little in their relationship God's way. It was a great moment for their marriage. They experienced a cleansing as they accepted God's judgment of their past. Even though they couldn't change the past, they could at long last be cleansed of it and begin to align themselves with God in every way they still could. What a cleansing! What repentance! What a liberation! This is what the gospel of Christ does.

Such an outcome may not occur every time we interact with a cohabiting couple, particularly those who are not yet Christians. Yet such remains the only acceptable goal: to see people repent of their sins, trust in Christ, be restored to obedience to God, and be changed forever. In the case of those guilty of sexual sin who were already professing Christians, Paul urged the church to call for their repentance and to seek their restoration to godly living. This was not to be done apart from deep love—it's clear that Paul loved this church. Rather, what Paul did, and what we must do, is show love to those who err by explaining God's better plan and show love toward God by upholding the truth of His Word.

Hebrews 13:4

This little verse comes in the last section of the letter to the Hebrews in the New Testament, which seems to be a list of reminders concerning the practicalities of Christian living. In this list we find a forthright word about marriage, marital sex, and nonmarital sex. About marriage the text states that it is "honorable." This interesting term in the rest of the New Testament refers to things that have enormous value, such as jewels, pearls, and other things of great cost. In the spiritual realm, *honorable* is used of the blood of Jesus, the promises of God, and saving faith in Christ—those things that have a value that is impossible to calculate, for they involve eternal realities.

The point is that God's ordinance of marriage occupies a lofty and precious place in His plan for humanity. Matrimony is, in fact, meant to be the foundation of all civilization, and the purposes of marriage have been much celebrated in the history of Christian theology. Marriage, first, provides intimate companionship for life (Gen. 2:18). Second, marriage was appointed by God for procreation and the loving, stable nurture of children (Eph. 6:1–2). Third, marriage provides a protected, safe, and fulfilling outlet for the human sex drive (1 Cor. 7:2). Finally, marriage, in both the Old and New Testaments, provides an abiding picture of God's covenantal love and salvation (Eph. 5:22–27). This image is significant because in it we are led to understand that entering into the relationship of marriage reflects our entrance into a relationship with God. Both provide peace, acceptance, and an unbreakable union.

Therefore the Bible has a narrow definition of marriage. A later chapter outlines the covenantal view of marriage—sealed by a vow to God that we will fulfill our marital responsibilities and obligations in order to foster over a lifetime a relationship of love and a godly heritage. Further, although routinely violated in today's world, the Bible commands married couples not to divorce, and proclaims that remarriage after divorce is adultery. Divorce is thought of in the Bible as a legal fiction because the wedding of two "selfs" in marriage creates a bond that cannot be severed. This holy, unbreakable union is what God meant to establish, and it calls for our utter respect. Marriage, once entered into, is from God's point of view a mandatory injunction for humanity, and is not to be dismissed for sexual, economic, or other reasons. It is fundamental for life. Dare we set it aside to do things our way?

A second point found in the text of Hebrews 13:4 is that the sexual relationship in marriage is "pure." The verse speaks of the "bed," which is a euphemism for the sexual relationship. The term used for purity refers to religious and moral purity. Thus, sex within marriage is a holy, positive, good thing with no hint or taint of sin or impurity. Sexual intimacy is God's gift to marriage. The covenant of marriage surrounds the intimate aspects of the marital relationship with God's blessing and the protection of trust and permanence, all of which allows that relationship to thrive. God intended the sexual relationship to be joined to the norm of marriage. This is violated at its core in cohabiting relationships.

Finally, this text injects a negative word about those who uncouple the sexual relationship from marriage, referring to them as "fornicators and adulterers." These two terms cover all who engage in nonmarital sex, the first referring to sex outside of marriage, the second referring to sexual relations that violate marriage vows. Cohabiters are squarely in the former category.

And God supplies a warning to such. With an astonishing abruptness, a simple statement is made about fornicators and adulterers—

God will judge them. What does this mean? Since the text is not specifically addressed to believers or unbelievers, one is given liberty to view this statement in a broad manner. God's judgment has many aspects in the Bible. One is temporal—God's judgment visited upon the disobedient in the form of natural consequences to sinful behavior. The incredible costs of sexual sin are evident all around us including, but not limited to, the moral darkening and slavery that sexual sin fosters. Perhaps we could view the subject of the preceding chapter—the consequences of cohabitation—as one aspect of God's judgment on sexual sin, taking note of all the unpleasant results that flow from the cohabiting lifestyle.

So part of God's judgment exists in the broken homes, the psychological and emotional pain, the violence, and all the rest, which are the natural consequences of not doing things God's way. Such consequences are the frequent partners of sexual sin, despite the many who consider cohabitation a benign lifestyle choice. Even believers can experience this form of God's judgment, and our experience of such outcomes should make us turn to God in repentance.

But God's judgment can go further than this. In the case of believers, judgment can be experienced in the form of God's chastisement. Believers who willfully sin against God will not receive eternal punishment (they've passed from death to life), but they are warned of God's severe discipline for persistent sin, including sexual sin (1 Cor. 5:1–5). The church, in fact, is called to have a role in discipline, leading one another to stay obedient to God. Believers should judge themselves, lest they fall into God's hands (1 Cor. 11:31–32). Sexual sin should not even be named as among Christians (Eph. 5:3).

The final aspect of God's judgment relates to unbelievers who fail to respect the ordinance of marriage. The Scripture condemns all those who seek to eliminate or disparage matrimony, whether by doctrine or behavior. Those who choose cohabitation do so in the face of God's ordinance. Cohabitation, however innocent and sincere its proponents allege it to be, is a rejection of God's ordinance and, therefore, a rejection and trivialization of God. God will judge those who seek their own path at the expense of His gifts to humanity, bringing His vengeance upon those who reject Him (1 Cor. 6:9). If a person rejects God, God will reject that person. That's the deal. Who today will deny that one of the chief avenues and manifestations of the rejection of God lies in the area of sexual morality? Unrepentant fornicators and adulterers are placed squarely among the damned. To go against God and His ordinance and remain in a faithless condition is to risk all of God's eternal wrath and damnation in hell (Rev. 21:8; 22:15). Many modern people no longer accept the concept of God's judgment and reject the doctrine of eternal punishment. Well, guess what? Modern people are not in charge—God is. And He promises a day of reckoning. The great need of many in our day is not the perfect relationship, not finding one's soul mate, but faith in Jesus Christ and His work on the cross for the forgiveness of sins. That's the *ultimate* need of every human being. We in pastoral work dare not lose sight of this.

It's clear, then, that the God-given moral code is purity of life in the premarital state and sexual faithfulness within marriage. Violation will bring enormous costs, including the many-faceted judgment and vengeance of God. This spiritual dimension of cohabitation is partner to the social dimension studied in previous chapters. In the latter case, cohabitation was proven to be an unwise, harmful course of behavior. In the former case, it is the rejection of God. The simple solution is to again return and recouple the God-given gift of intimate sexuality with the norm of marriage.

What enormous problems would be solved if this simple rule were followed! Much of American society today persists in a godless infatuation with the cohabiting relationship. Given the consequences, it's vital that a renewed ideal of marriage and sexuality be returned to the minds and hearts of men and women. Moreover, it seems clear that Bible-believing and teaching pastors should be on the front lines of this effort.

This chapter began by talking about couples who come to me for weddings. Sometimes they don't have a relationship with God and are in a cohabiting situation. I try to deal with them gently, speaking the truth to them, while giving them the opportunity to come into a relationship with God through faith in Christ. But sometimes couples come to me claiming to be Christians, claiming to have experienced the new birth, claiming to have a relationship with God, yet nonetheless engaged in cohabitation. I try to help them see how such a lifestyle is utterly incompatible with the Christian faith. In no way, shape, or form should a professing Christian be found cohabiting. According to the great apostle, it should not even be named as among us!

On Thursday, June 19, 1997, I heard Dr. Laura Schlesinger, the popular radio therapist, receive a call from a woman in her early thirties. Her live-in companion wanted to buy a house, but he wanted to place the house in his name only. Dr. Laura takes a dim view of cohabitation, and she focused the conversation on why the woman's boyfriend would not share title to the house with her. According to the woman, it was because she'd walked out on him briefly two years earlier, and there was some doubt in his mind that she'd stay with him, despite their having lived together for the better part of thirteen years. Dr. Laura inquired about this breakup. The woman replied that she'd become a Christian two years earlier and subsequently had doubts about the wisdom and morality of the relationship. So, for a time, she left him.

Dr. Laura, an orthodox, observant Jew, erupted into a spasm of incredulity. "Wait a minute," she said, "shacking up and being a Christian do not go together! If you talk it, you have to walk it!" Barely audible, the woman muttered, "I know." By the end of the conversation she seemed encouraged to make some better decisions in her life.

Can we not see that if a person claims to know and follow Christ, the sum and substance of pastoral work and all pastoral counseling is to move this person into obedience to God? How can a Christian experience the fullness of the Holy Spirit and the wholeness of life in the body of Christ while compromised by a sinful lifestyle?

Despite its casual acceptance today, pastors, as those charged with teaching God's truth to others, should have no uncertainty about what Scripture teaches regarding cohabitation. Let's load these aspects of God's truth into our theological arsenal and fight the good fight of speaking the truth in love. Once the utter wrongness of cohabitation is settled in our minds and hearts, it is left only to pursue the deep and powerful meaning of marriage as presented in the Bible. What, though, does the other path look like?

PART 2

Marriage

┠─────────────────────────────────

Chapter 7

Marriage as a
Covenant in the Bible

A great deal of attention was generated a few years ago concerning the so-called "covenant marriage law" in Louisiana. This law, which went into effect on August 15, 1997, amended divorce and marriage statutes with the aim of causing premarital couples to take a more serious view of the commitment of marriage. The law stipulates that when a couple chooses the option of a covenant marriage (it's not mandatory), a certain pledge or declaration must be made at the time of marriage. This pledge affirms that marriage is a "lifelong relationship," and couples must submit an affidavit stating that they've received premarital counseling and carry a notarized attestation from a member of the clergy or a counselor.

Equally significant is the divorce provision of the law. In order for a divorce to be granted, the presence of a "total breach" must be established under a few proven grounds such as adultery, felony conviction, abandonment, physical or sexual abuse, or cruelty. In addition, a separation provision is included, designating a time period that must expire prior to any divorce, during which the couple must seek marital counseling. This law was directed more at the divorce problem than at the cohabitation problem, but it recognizes the need to restore at the outset of marriage a better understanding of marital commitment. A few other states have also considered this kind of legislation.

Many parties have weighed in with their thoughts concerning this type of provision. Dr. Laura Schlesinger loved it, and devoted a monologue to it on one of her programs. Also, the *NBC Today* show featured a debate between a sponsoring legislator from Louisiana and a feminist lawyer from New York.[1] The latter was dead set against it, believing it would doom women to abusive relationships. Her solution to the divorce problem was teaching communication skills, beginning as early as the third or fourth grade. The *Wall Street Journal* weighed in also, carrying some pieces praising the concept of a covenant marriage law. Those opinion pieces elicited a number of critical letters to the editor.[2]

Most of the letter writers felt that the covenant marriage law was a bad idea for several reasons: it was an unwarranted intrusion of the government into the business of families, that it would discriminate against the poor, that no-fault laws do not cause divorces, that it was an enshrinement of religious dogma, and that it would cause people to remain in unhappy or abusive marriages. Finally, syndicated newspaper columnist Clarence Page expressed dislike for the law because it would make those choosing noncovenant marriages feel "cheap and flighty."[3] Although unsettled by the divorce rate, Page had doubts that this law was the solution.

He may have a point. There is, after all, no mention of God in the new law. The explanation of the term covenant is actually quite secular. The addition of the term *covenant* to the marriage laws of Louisiana seems rather a feel-good measure that merely gives cosmetic dressing to a statute that essentially stiffens divorce laws. The attempt to raise awareness and commitment at the initiation of a marriage through the pledge and the counseling provision is laudable, but in no sense does this law expound and declare the power, beauty, and meaning of a true biblical covenant. Such is what this chapter presents.

Part 2 of this book talks about marriage. And that means beginning with the concept of covenant, a concept that must be derived from the Bible. It seems unwise to leave the teaching of the biblical doctrine of covenant to the state legislatures of our land. The present purpose, then, is to acquaint the reader with a biblical and historical understanding of the covenant of marriage. This understanding must be regained in order to restore a proper understanding of holy matrimony.

One of the problems discussed throughout this book is the diminished significance of marriage in our culture. We're beginning to see that the alternatives we've sought for marriage are proving to be very bad medicine, indeed. So, in order to restore the proper place of marriage and the proper understanding of marriage, it's necessary to address the serious covenantalism of the Bible. Part 1 of this book studied the conclusions of social science research regarding cohabitation. Part 2 now turns to the Scriptures for an understanding of just what God intended marriage to be.

Covenant: The Biblical Term

The Hebrew word for covenant *(berit)* is used more than 280 times in the Old Testament. It's never used as a verb, only as a noun, although the phrase "to cut a covenant" appears frequently. The root or origin of the word is not known for certain, but there's no question about what it came to mean in Bible usage.

In the ancient world, a covenant was used to strike a bargain. But it included more than a bargain. It actually established a relationship between the parties who struck the bargain. Given the lack of organized legal institutions and the difficulty of enforcing agreements in the ancient world, this mechanism of using covenants developed. In our society, I might strike a bargain with a painter to paint my house. I might give him half the money at the start and the other half when the job is done. If he never does the work, and refuses to return my money, I can take him to court to force him to pay. If he does the work and I don't pay him the rest of what is owed, he can take me to court and force me to pay. No such legal recourse existed in the ancient world, so covenants were developed.

A covenant was at that time a special kind of agreement between parties who established a relationship—a relationship that carried with it certain specified obligations. The covenant was sealed by some act or sign, which invoked God as the "enforcer" of the agreement.

Definitions of *covenant* abound. One simple definition that captures the meaning of the term is "an elective relationship of obligation under divine sanction."[4] Another good definition is "a pledge or agreement . . . with obligations . . . accompanied by signs, sacrifices, and a solemn oath that sealed the relationship with curses and blessings."[5] The basic idea of a covenant, then, is that of establishing a relationship that carries with it obligations under the watchful eye of God. The vocabulary used in association with the word *covenant* in the Bible illuminates the intent of establishing a covenant. One can cut, set, give, arrange, establish, or enter a covenant. And one is to keep, remember, observe, or hold fast to it. One should not break, transgress, sin against, forsake, despise, or forget the covenant one has made.[6]

In the Bible the ceremonies that sealed a covenant were many, including animal sacrifice, the erection of a monument, sharing a common meal, exchanging of gifts, oaths, libations, and so forth. An oath statement of some kind often accompanied the ratification of a covenant. It's clear, then, that a covenant was meant to be serious business. Once the covenant was established, the parties to the agreement were obligated to carry out their respective commitments, with the understanding that God would bless them if they did so and would punish them if they did not.

Covenants could be made between individuals, between nations, and between God and humanity. Friends as well as enemies entered

into them. Covenants could be simple, personal agreements or elaborate treaties. Examples abound in the Bible. God, for instance, made
a covenant with Abraham, obligating Himself to make him the father
of many nations (Gen. 17:1–8), and the sign of the covenant was cir-
cumcision. Jonathan and David made a covenant, assigning Jonathan
the obligation of protecting David from King Saul (1 Sam. 18:3–4).
They exchanged possessions to seal the covenant. In Jeremiah 34:8,
King Zedekiah led the nation of Israel in a covenant to renew their
obedience to God's Word, a covenant that was soon violated. And it
is widely acknowledged, of course, that the entire structure of God's
relationship to His chosen people, Israel, follows the outline of a covenant. God was both a party to this covenant and the guarantor of it;
He was both witness and participant. In the last century, scholars like
Mendenhall demonstrated this spiritual understanding of covenant.[7]
These sacred agreements were used to express relationships "all
through the two millennia of ancient Near Eastern history."[8]

Several elements of a covenant can be seen from Scripture. First
there is *intent*. The parties purposely enter a relationship that demands
obligations, and agree to them. Next there are *vows* or solemn words
that give utterance to the intent. Often the *obligations* of each party
were spelled out and, most importantly, *the presence of God* was acknowledged. God stands over the agreement to enforce the obligations. Then a *sign,* some physical act, ratified the agreement.

So a covenant is a solemn, sacred agreement, in which persons bind
themselves to certain obligations, swearing an oath and signifying in a
ceremony the total commitment to fulfill the obligations. The promise is made under God's watchful eye. He is the witness as to whether
the obligations are completed or not, and curses or blessings flow ac-
cordingly. These agreements are not meant to be entered into lightly.

It's revealing, indeed, that in the Bible, marriage is presented as a
covenant! Many wonder at some of the modern wedding customs
commonly practiced: the stating of vows, the ceremony of the rings,
and the elaborate promises. Most of these traditions have been handed

down from the past, when there was a greater understanding of the covenantalism of marriage.

But the sign of marriage, according to many Bible scholars, is not the exchange of rings or the lighting of a unity candle but rather the consummation of the marriage with physical intimacy. This act was meant by God to mark the decisive end to the premarital state. The sexual act's possessing this exalted purpose, little wonder that premarital sex weakens subsequent marriages. It reaches into the future and robs something from the covenant. Part of the glue that binds couples in marriage is missing when sexual intimacy has come long before the marriage. Nonmarital sex, therefore, is a pretense since it cannot form a true union. The sexual experience itself has no power to bind. Only when a covenant of marriage surrounds sexual intimacy does it have the power to deepen the bond. And all of these elements together—intent, vows, obligation, sign, and that most important presence of God—finally form a new *relationship* that did not exist before. It is this understanding we must restore.

Given the significance of the biblical concept of covenant, the gravity of the marital relationship as a sacred covenant should become clear. Equally grave is the realization of how far modern society has drifted from the lofty notion of marriage as a covenant.

Marriage as Covenant in the Bible

Nancy was a typically modern person. She finished her education and began her career. At some point she decided to get serious about finding a husband. She finally found Mr. Right—Rob—and wedding plans were made. Although Nancy and Rob didn't cohabit prior to their marriage, the whole time she prepared for her wedding, Nancy thought, *If this doesn't work out, I am going to get out of it.* She, like many in our society today, felt it was important to always keep her options open. So she married Rob with this typically modern way of looking at matrimony, saying, "I'm committed to this man enough to marry him, but not necessarily enough to stay with him, if things don't work out the way I want them to." Today, many people approach marriage this way.

Some years later, Nancy and Rob came to faith in Jesus Christ and subsequently fell under the teaching of God's Word. Nancy found that the Bible holds out a totally different understanding of the commitment of marriage, often given expression by the lovely language of a traditional wedding ceremony. A couple promises "to have and to hold from this day forth, for better and for worse, in sickness and in health, for richer and for poorer, until death do us part" or other similar words. Nancy later came to realize how her earlier attitude might have become a self-fulfilling prophecy had God not changed her heart, leading her to strengthen her commitment to her marriage. She and Rob renewed their wedding vows, and this time she really meant them. She, therefore, fulfilled the spirit of a covenant. It is this understanding—the spirit of covenant—that pastors must restore to their flocks.

Some passages in the Bible explicitly state that marriage is a covenant. Other passages do not mention the term covenant but still reflect the covenantal meaning. Following are some of these passages.

Malachi 2:14–16

In this well-known passage, God rebukes the husbands in Israel who were divorcing their wives after many years of marriage. God reminded them that their wives were their "companions," and the "wives of [their] youth," and the "wives of [their] covenant." And God reminded them that He was the witness to their covenant of marriage. Therefore what the men had done was an offense to God Himself, who was part of the covenant. God had made them "one," an allusion to Genesis 2:24 when Adam and Eve became "one flesh" in the first "marriage" in history. God does not view marriage as some kind of private, contractual agreement that can be dissolved when anyone feels like it. He views marriage as a sacred obligation. God thus made it clear in the Malachi passage that He was bringing chastisement upon the nation because of their actions. In this, God was fulfilling His role as a partner in the covenant.

Ezekiel 16:8

This text comes in the midst of a long allegory, in which God compares the nation of Israel to an abandoned orphan girl. The orphan girl was rescued and became the privileged wife of a king, only to throw it all away and become a prostitute. The story is analogous to God's rescuing Israel and making them the apple of His eye, only to have them turn to false gods and idols. Thus, both the orphan girl and Israel were unfaithful to their covenants. God reminded Israel that He had sworn an oath to them to be their God. And the orphan girl had made the solemn promises of a marriage covenant. In the teaching of the Bible, marriage is a covenant that parallels God's covenant with His people. So I always remind the congregation gathered for weddings that every marriage is a metaphor of what it means to have a relationship with God. It pictures the indissoluble bond between God and His children, and Christ and His church. Marriage reflects these sacred bonds—but it has been terribly profaned in our times.

Proverbs 2:17

This little piece of "wisdom" is a warning against the wayward woman, a woman willing to pursue a man who is not her husband. The text says she is a woman who has forsaken the "companion of her youth," that is, her husband, and in doing so, she's forgotten "the covenant of her God." God is present in every marriage, the third strand of the marriage braid, binding two people together. Violating the covenant of marriage is a serious sin against what is holy.

Genesis 2:21–25

This text is, of course, foundational for the imagery of marriage in the Bible. Both the Lord Jesus Christ and the apostle Paul returned to it when instructing us about marriage. Not only does this passage show God's direct act in establishing marriage, it also sets forth Adam and Eve as the prototype of all marital partners in that they became "one flesh." Adam stated, in fact, that the woman had become his "flesh and bone." Elsewhere in the Old Testament this phrase refers to the kinship union of relatives, indicating that marriage creates between two previously unrelated people a bond of family where none existed before (Gen. 29:14; Judg. 9:2; 2 Sam. 5:1; 19:13; 1 Chron. 11:1). This bond is what Jesus referred to when He said, "Therefore, what God has joined together, let not man separate" (Mark 10:9). Divorce attempts to sever something that can never really be severed, which explains why it's so painful. Marriage creates a union, an indissoluble bond, and such is how we are to view our marriages.

Many other passages serve to illustrate the spiritual state of marriage, but these give us the flavor of marriage as a covenant. Showers sets forth the conclusive arguments summarizing why marriage is to be viewed as a biblical covenant:

1. The Bible contains straightforward statements that marriage is a covenant.
2. The word *covenant* is used of marriage.
3. Marriage is marked out within the covenantal structure of God's relationship to Israel (e.g., Deut. 22:22–29).
4. The Old Testament covenant between God and Israel parallels the covenant of marriage.
5. The New Testament covenantal relationship of Christ and the church pictures the marriage relationship.[9]

Thus, it's important to distinguish marriage from other legal contracts. Marriage is not a mere legality or contractual agreement, something we can form and break casually. God's hand is, after all, in the establishment of the marriage bond, making it sacred as formed and witnessed by Him. Experience demonstrates the pain of ripping apart something not meant to ever come apart.

Some years ago a church had fallen on hard financial times. The country was in a recession, people in the church had been thrown out of work, and the church coffers were growing empty. The congregation held an emergency meeting to decide what to spend money on and what to cut. Discussion moved on to the support of the church's missionaries—the Christian workers the church had promised to support financially as they took the gospel to other lands. One church leader arose and said, "We can't cut the support of the missionaries; our promise to them is like a wedding vow!" He meant that the church's commitment to support these workers overseas was a sacred obligation and, therefore, irrevocable, not something that could be set aside. That this man used the comparison he did is illustrative of the importance of the marriage covenant. No other analogy can so capture the spirit of an unbreakable promise than the words "wedding vow."

Where has this thinking gone in our society? It seems that it's all but disappeared in our marriage-disposing culture. There's a great need, however, to restore the biblical understanding of marriage as a covenant. It must be restored first in the church and then all across the broader land. And pastors must lead the effort as those who proclaim God's truth and are entrusted with the nurturing of marriages and families. Marriage is, of course, a human right, natural to all humanity and older than the church. Although pastors don't have jurisdiction over every marriage, those couples who do come to the church for a wedding must be taught that marriage involves a sacred promise to God, a promise that is larger than the two people who make it.

When some of those in our charge grow weary of their marriages we must remind them of the vow they've made. Yes, there are times when people will grow unhappy in their marriages. But what is happiness? It comes and it goes. And as it has gone, it will often, in time, return again. A covenant of marriage helps people to keep their vows during those times when they may not feel like it. Thus, there are times when we keep our vows and there are times when our vows keep us. A husband and wife need to live in awareness, then, of the covenantal bond they've established.

This lack of a bond is perhaps part of the reason why 80 percent of the time unions formed upon the foundation of cohabitation don't work out. With no bond, there's no glue to help a couple stick together when things are difficult. Cohabiting relationships are often formed, in fact, with the specific intention that there be no glue. Even if a subsequent marriage takes place, often the concept of covenant is not part of the equation, God not part of the commitment. Should we wonder, then, that these relationships seldom work out? And equally troublesome in cohabiting relationships, sexual intimacy is uncoupled from the commitment of marriage, further weakening any subsequent marriage bond. The simple truth is that the practice of cohabitation does not follow God's wisdom on how to establish permanent love relationships. Little wonder they fail at the rate they do.

In a recent "Dear Abby" column, a twenty-year-old woman wrote to Abby seeking some advice.[10] She explained that she'd been living with her boyfriend over the last year in a one-bedroom apartment. The arrangement included not only the cohabiting couple but also the father of the boyfriend. This woman wanted, for obvious reasons, to get their own place. The boyfriend, however, was not ready to leave the "nest," arguing that the couple had it made, living there rent free. She despaired leaving this fellow because "every time we kiss, it's like the first time." What crazy predicaments people get into when they fail to understand the nature of marriage and God's instructions pertaining to this holy ordinance!

One can only wonder about the millions of cohabiting couples across our land. In what kind of arrangements do they live? What are the real motives behind these relationships? And how unlikely is it that such arrangements will turn out to be happy and blessed experiences? Certainly these couples are sorely in need of God's wisdom on love and marriage.

Chapter 8

The Marriage Covenant in Christian History

It's shocking to realize how far our culture's view of marriage has fallen. The "Arts and Ideas" section of the *New York Times* recently asked a handful of academics to offer suggestions for the most overrated ideas. Two law professors nominated marriage as overrated. They said,

> Marriage is not only overrated in our society, but also overworked as a panacea. Politicians offer marriage as social policy and as the cure for child poverty and other social ills. . . . Building stable families, however, should not be primarily about rescuing marriage. Families come in different forms, held together by many types of ties. . . . Why should our policy privilege marriage over these other family ties? Historically, marital families were assumed to be good for children, but in our post-sexual-revolution world of gender equality and no-fault divorce, reliance on marriage seems naïve.[1]

One of the aims of this book is to help us recover a biblical view of marriage, to resist the declining view of marriage in our society. We must resist the notion that something like cohabitation is an acceptable or positive alternative to marriage. Cohabitation is not marriage and marriage is not cohabitation. This distinction has always been made in the history of the church until only recently. This chapter reflects the need, especially among pastors, to regain this sense of history. What follows, then, outlines some of the doctrinal developments on marriage over the various eras of church history.

Although the church's view of marriage has not always been entirely biblical, it has never, historically speaking, accepted cohabitation as having moral equivalence with marriage. Some voices in the modern, liberal church (more on them later) seek this moral equivalence, but for the most part, the church has held to the uniqueness of marriage. And when the church has been at its best, it has expounded and taught the depth and power of the marriage covenant.

Even earlier than in the church, we can find some illuminating practices surrounding the wedding event in ancient Jewish law and custom. First, a binding agreement establishing a betrothal period prior to the wedding was struck between the family of the groom and the family of the bride. The groom usually paid a sum of money to the bride's father, called a bride-price. The bride was often endowed with a gift from her family, called a dowry. It later became traditional for the bride-price to also be passed on to the couple, with the provision that it would revert to the bride and her family should the man ever divorce his wife. All these provisions were spelled out in the *Ketubah,* the signed wedding document that governed the transaction. The purpose of these financial arrangements was to create economic incentives to stay in the bond of marriage once it was entered. Financial benefits flowed to those who got married and those who stayed married. Financial loss came to those who eschewed marriage or who left marriages.

Ancient people seemed to be smarter than we in the modern world. Three thousand years ago, Jewish law was established to help provide stability for marriages. In studying the history of the church, much the same spirit can be found. That is, until recent times.

The Early Church

The early church grew up in the Roman world, and Roman law had very lengthy and complex provisions concerning matrimony. Marriage was sharply distinguished from other unions, since the legitimacy of offspring, inheritance questions, class status, property rights, and so forth were bound up with the decisions people made concerning marriage and family. Thus, even in ancient Rome it was not possible from a legal standpoint to equate cohabitation with marriage. Cohabitation, however, was quite common; Roman law prohibited marriage between classes, leading to a common practice of interclass cohabitation.[2] As Christian influence grew in the empire over the centuries, the distinction between marriage and cohabitation was strengthened for moral reasons. Although Roman law was never totally "Christianized," it was influenced by the moral perspective of the church.

The church, however, developed its own body of teaching concerning marriage. The earliest Christian literature did not give in-depth treatment to the subject of marriage, but what was written affirmed its goodness and sacredness. In the early centuries of the Christian faith, the church did not presume to have jurisdiction over the marriages of its members as it later came to be practiced, so wedding liturgies and rites did not exist. They came later in the medieval period. Some early theologians such as Tertullian argued, in language consistent with a covenantal view of marriage, that marriage formed an unbreakable bond.[3] John Chrysostum later said that a man should not merely live with his wife but "be joined" to her to show a complete union and intense love.[4] Tertullian and others before him, including Ignatius, argued that couples ought to come to their local pastor (bishop) to seek approval of their nuptials, which allowed the church to teach young people the biblical view of marriage. Nowhere in all my reading and research did I find one early church apologist or theologian who judged a convenient sexual relationship to be the same as marriage. Such a thing was foreign to their mind-set.

Augustine, the great theologian and bishop of Hippo, became the first Christian to write extensively on marriage. Augustine labored to articulate the biblical view of marriage in its full light. Most agree that to some extent he succeeded, despite an overly negative view of marital sex. Below is a summary of his views, following which are some relevant facts about his life—quite a story in light of the subject of this book.

Augustine saw three goods in marriage: the faithful union of two partners, which channeled sexual desire in its proper direction; procreation, including the education and nurture of children; and what he called "sacrament," by which he meant the mystical connection of marriage to the greater bond between Christ and the church. In this latter he saw the sacred aspect of the marriage bond. Augustine did not use the term covenant to refer to marriage, but his concept of "sacrament" included the idea of an oathed bond that symbolized the union between Christ and the church, forming an indissoluble bond. His ideas were, therefore, consistent with the biblical notion of covenant.

Of great interest is Augustine's life. In his *Confessions* Augustine made no secret of his past as a heretic and a fornicator (as he would have undoubtedly described himself). Prior to his conversion, Augustine, all through his younger manhood, lived with a woman apart from marriage. He admitted that the final and perhaps greatest resistance he found in surrendering to the gospel was not his intellectual difficulties with the faith, but the simple sin of lust. He didn't want to give up this union and the pleasure of its sexual relationship. And this barrier was the last to fall. It was curious that he long desired marriage but all the while merely lived with this woman who was apparently, for whatever reason (probably class), not suitable for marriage. He could not or would not marry her even though he loved her and fathered a beloved son by her. She was heartbroken when, prior to his conversion, Augustine parted from her. When Augustine did finally come to Christ at age thirty-one, he swore off both fornication and marriage, and became celibate.

Given his experience, Augustine understood the power of lust, the pleasure of sex, and their connection to spiritual commitment. He also had a high view of marriage, both before his conversion and after. In his *Confessions,* Augustine reported that his sainted mother saw him converted. His own son, borne of his lust (as he would say it), was converted and ushered to heaven prematurely. And he himself became a great teacher of the faith. Augustine understood, both by way of study and by way of experience, many things about the issues discussed in this book. If he were around today, he'd certainly do a better job authoring a volume like this. He understood what marriage was and what marriage was not. Before the sociological term was employed, he understood what cohabitation was and what it was not.

The previous chapter developed the great and lofty truth of the marriage covenant. Such a fresh study of the Bible raises the tattered and wearied institution of marriage from its travails in this world to the most sacred of dimensions. Marriage is a divine gift, where two unrelated souls, man and woman, embrace one another in holy covenant, joined by God, pledging to be faithful and loving, partnering to be lifelong companions under the watchful eye of God, until death parts them. It is at once both the greatest good and the greatest challenge. Can a man or woman do a greater thing than to remain loving and faithful to his or her marriage partner until death? What is greater than finishing what one starts and finishing it well? What is more holy or scriptural than keeping a covenant?

What, on the other hand, is cohabitation? In whatever form it occurs, however much love and caring is found within it, whatever reason is uttered in its defense, however common it has become, it remains, as Augustine so aptly put it, a "bargain struck for lust."[5] That was his personal conclusion, looking back on his own life. *A bargain struck for lust.* Nothing more, nothing less. It is not marriage. It is not holy. It is not sacred. It is not a covenant. It is not God's plan. It forms no bond. It is a pale and profane arrangement. Augustine knew all this because he lived it. Such was the understanding of the greatest thinker and writer of the early church. I'm humbled to associate my own views with his. Marriage is the better way, and I pray our modern world will rediscover this.

The Medieval Period

Church authority over marriage reached its zenith in the medieval period. By the eleventh century, couples in the Christian world understood that a marriage would be valid only if it was enacted within the domain of the church, in the proper liturgical form. Gradually, as it's been put, the church moved from blessing the bond to creating the knot.[6] This had the unfortunate result of thrusting the church into the endless problem of determining which marriages were valid and which were not, since many people continued to marry outside the sphere of the church. When these couples later attached themselves to the church, the church felt it had to wrestle with whether or not these unsanctioned marriages, called "clandestine marriages," were valid. The covenantal view of marriage was therefore obscured by the church's excessive regulatory practices regarding it. Although the covenantal doctrine of marriage during this period was eclipsed somewhat by these regulatory concerns, there's no hint that the church saw lesser unions, such as cohabitation, on the same plane as marriage.

Marriage was still seen as a sacramental, indissoluble bond, and a clear distinction was maintained between marriage and all forms of fornication, including cohabitation and concubinage. The error made in this period was to wed the notion of an indissoluble bond to the church's authority to grant sacramental status to a marriage, rather than to the simple notion of a biblical covenant. The church couldn't bring itself to acknowledge any marriage outside of itself, although clearly, based on the Bible, marriage must be seen as a human reality, older than the church. So a formalistic and legalistic rule replaced the beauty of covenantalism. The sacramental view of marriage did, however, uphold covenantal ideas of the marriage bond.

The Reformers

When Martin Luther married the former nun Katharina von Bora on June 13, 1525, likely no one was more surprised than he. He'd been raised under a system that extolled celibacy above marriage, and taken and kept monastic vows for twenty years. When he finally married, he was forty-two years old. Some critics of Luther have asserted that his personal desire for marriage was one of the motives for leading the Reformation. This charge is patently false. A lapse of some years ensued between the time that his Protestant convictions emerged and the time of his marriage. Too, attention to Luther's writings shows his commitment to the Scriptures; he had no interest in a justification for his own personal behavior. According to Luther himself, if there were any nonromantic reason for his marriage, it was to "spite the devil."[7]

In the days succeeding the publication of his views on celibacy and marriage, Luther had to cope with personal attacks and rumors (such as that Katie was pregnant before the nuptials). By most accounts, he had a happy marriage, despite these attacks. Luther's views on marriage matured over time and his ample writings on the subject leave little doubt where he stood. His thinking and the thinking of other Reformers will be considered below. It's important to note, however, that the Reformers did not develop a systematic doctrine on marriage; their work was primarily pastoral, since they were acutely occupied with pastoral work. Luther's concern, in particular, was to set free "bewildered consciences."[8]

Luther rejected the idea that the church ought to govern the legalities of marriage. Marriage was a natural right, not an ecclesiastical function. He believed, as do I, that marriages outside of the church are no more or less sacred than marriages inside of the church.[9] Marriages are sacred not because we ascribe sacredness to them, but because God witnesses them, wherever and however they are solemnized. This view did not prevent Luther from extolling marriage as a sacred calling and he was not averse to participating in weddings and "blessing" the union of Christian couples. He even authored a wedding liturgy for other pastors, feeling that pastors had a responsibility to instruct and pray for people entering marriage.

Although Luther did not emphasize the covenantal view of marriage, he did at times refer to marriage as a covenant.[10] And his views reflected the profound simplicity of the Bible's teaching on marriage. All of his teaching and pastoral work was built on the idea that marriage is a sacred bond to be reverenced and nurtured. He clearly opposed other questionable relationships and was a man of marriage to the core.

The great Swiss Reformer John Calvin had similar views. He also referred to marriage in covenantal terms and encouraged, like Luther, a fresh biblical and pastoral view of marriage in the church. These two reformation leaders, for all their great intellectual abilities, had a profoundly simple view of marriage: it was of God. They stood on plain biblical instruction and pastored the flocks under their care. Neither wrote an elaborate theology of marriage but they grasped that marriage was a bond for life sealed by God. And they pressed their people to embrace this understanding. In no sense did the Reformers lower or compromise the distinctiveness of marriage versus alternatives such as cohabitation. Such other arrangements were held to be sinful.

The Puritan Movement

The Puritans were so called because of their desire, beginning in sixteenth-century England, to reform the church, making it "pure" from all trappings of High Church Anglicanism and any influences of Roman Catholicism. A movement that extended into the seventeenth century, Puritanism began in England but found its way to America. A popular movement, it cut across sects and denominations, including such groups as Presbyterians, Baptists, and Congregationalists.[11] The movement included many prominent churchmen whose very biblical writings are abundantly available today.

The popular notion that all Puritans were hostile to pleasure is not born out by the facts, which most scholars now recognize. The Puritans were strict, championing discipline and self-control, but they also sought to openly enjoy God's good and holy gifts. They held a high view of marital love and taught more openly of the sexual dimension of marriage than churchmen had for centuries. Their concurrent high view of both virginity and marital intimacy is not unlike the view held by many evangelicals today. Puritan views are so important to us because of the deep impact the Puritan movement made in the shaping of early American history. One historian has said that "Puritanism . . . was firmly rooted in the American experience and in the emerging American mind. . . . It has radiated its influence in American civilization, for good or ill, from that day to this; and the end is not yet."[12] Puritan teaching on marriage marked a decisive return to understanding marriage as a covenant in its full biblical sense.

The Puritans ultimately believed that God gave marriage as a gift to rescue man from loneliness (Gen. 2:18). The highest good of marriage was seen, therefore, as intimate companionship, within the confines of a covenantal love and mutual obligation to one another. To the Puritans, the sexual dimension of marriage was simply the highest aspect of marital love and companionship. They believed in a healthy pursuit of marital happiness, and the movement, as a whole, manifested this holy aim. In this the Puritans had rediscovered the biblical teaching of marriage.

The covenant of marriage carried with it duties that were not ends in themselves but were designed to cause the continuing health of the bond. Thus, the commitment of marriage was not a sterile duty to merely persevere through the years but was meant for couples to fully engage in the enjoyment of a life together. So the duties of marriage were pursued with vigor by Puritan preachers. One Puritan writer authored a volume of some six hundred pages on this subject titled *Of Domesticall Duties*.[13] The theme of the work was how to follow through on marital love over a lifetime. The Puritan movement sought, then, to nurture marriages, not just form them.

In the theological sense, Puritans understood the divine participation in the covenant of marriage. Marriage was an indissoluble bond, not because it was a sacrament but because God formed the union. Early New England laws, under the influence of the Puritans, were fashioned in such a way so as to protect marriage. Clandestine marriages and forms of cohabitation were virtually outlawed.

Some brief quotes from actual Puritan writings illumine their high view of marriage and marital love:

> All other agreements and contracts made by mutuall consent may be broken and dissolved by the like consent of both parties: but in the contract of marriage, Almightie God commeth in as a witness; yea, he receiveth the promise of both parties, as joyning them in that estate. . . . Wedlocke or Matrimonie, is a lawful knot, and unto God an acceptable yoking and joyning together of one man, and one woman, with the good consent of them both. . . . It is a coupling together of two persons into one flesh, not to be broken, according unto the ordinance of God, so to continue during the life of either of them.[14]

> The great God commands thee to love her, how vile are those who don't love their wives.[15]

> My sweet spouse, let us delight in the love of each other as the chief of all earthly comforts.[16]

Far from diminishing marital pleasure, Puritan beliefs offer proofs that they enjoyed strong and ardent romance in their marriages. They saw the trust produced by the covenant of marriage as that which allowed the growth and excitement of marital love.

The Puritan era, therefore, building on the Reformers, marked a decisive return to the biblical and covenantal view of marriage. The Puritan biblicism allowed the fresh rediscovery of what God intended marriage to be. They expounded positively the goodness of marriage and the enjoyment of marital love. With this they maintained a sorrowful disapproval of adultery, cohabitation, and other forms of sexual sin, which they felt would wound body and spirit. The Puritans were, without doubt, like any other group of people, some having good marriages and some struggling. But without question the Puritans created a climate in which the commitment and obligations of marriage could thrive. This climate may, at least in part, explain the tremendous stability of the American family over the first two centuries of our history. Not until more recently has the American family begun to disintegrate even as the covenantal view of marriage came under attack.

The Modern Era

The Puritan view of marriage became the dominant one for most of American history. Research of published sermons on the subject of marriage over the first two hundred years of American history finds the covenantal view of marriage being consistently taught to people from the pulpits of our land. Such was true across denominational and regional lines.

As late as 1909, for example, Stuart Lawrence Tyson, a professor at the University of the South in Nashville, published a lecture, endorsed by the bishop of his denomination, titled "The Teaching of Our Lord as to the Indissolubility of Marriage." In this lecture, Tyson strongly argued for aspects of the covenantal view of marriage, even though the volume is riddled with a higher critical view of Scripture. Higher criticism, which gained prominence beginning in the nineteenth century, eventually undid many of the great doctrines of biblical Christianity but was apparently not fully applied to the doctrine of marriage. A high view of marriage was proclaimed even in the absence of a high view of

Scripture, which gives evidence of how profoundly indoctrinated American society was in the Puritan view of marriage. References to the covenant view of marriage can, in fact, be found in school textbooks, magazines, and other material oriented to the popular culture. As late as 1959 a book of sermons published by the National Council of Churches, America's most well-known bastion of liberal theology, contains a sermon on marriage that makes a strong presentation of the covenantal view. The sermon argued that marriage "is a physical and spiritual union ordained by God to fulfill His purpose, a sacred unity therefore that must not be broken."[17] It's remarkable that now, just a few decades later, totally new and radical definitions of marriage, the family, and sexual morality are being embraced not only outside the church but inside it as well.

The Puritan view, however, held sway for a long time. Despite the doctrinal shifts that have occurred in American Christianity since the time of the Puritans—particularly in the large, mainline denominations—a similar shift regarding the theology of marriage did not take place, for the most part, until recent decades. It's not surprising that the traditional view of marriage parallels a period of relative stability, culturally speaking, for the American family, when divorce and cohabitation rates were low.

A word should be said about Karl Barth, whose writings appeared in the early and middle twentieth century. Barth is a well-known theologian, often considered the father of what is called neoorthodox theology. Among its other positions, neoorthodoxy does not hold to the inerrancy and infallibility of Scripture. Still, although Barth held a relatively low view of the trustworthiness of Scripture, in his extended treatment of marriage, Barth states that it must be seen as under the "divine command."[18] It is God's ordinance. Barth demonstrates that the Lord Jesus expressed Himself clearly on the "indissolubility and the sanctity of marriage."[19] The covenant creates the obligation of love within the context of exclusive monogamy. Barth emphatically states that "to enter upon marriage is to renounce the possibility of leaving it."[20] This sounds very Puritan. Barth's treatment is considerably more passionate than one might expect, and contains pastoral remarks about the need to choose a marriage partner wisely. He points to God's grace, which operates so that even though "man does not keep the command, the command keeps man."[21] Barth's passion was conveyed by his eloquent dismissal of relationships that do not conform to the biblical ideal of covenant marriage:

> . . . [this] is playing at love. . . . Is it really good, is it ever convenient and reassuring, to be able and even to have to reckon with the constant possibility of a rupture (very likely from the other side), to be released from and therefore deprived of the seriousness of the whole relationship? But the question can be posed in other terms, namely whether a relationship of love and marriage which reckons seriously with the possibility of rupture is conceivable at all and is not a *mad illusion*. . . . The idea of a trial marriage or provisional association, and therefore the whole idea of a temporary marriage, can never do justice to this inherent feature of every such relationship. If we take these ideas seriously, if we work out all their implications, we shall certainly come up against the fact that behind them there stands as their *essential truth* the idea of permanent fellowship. (emphasis added)[22]

Thus, for a long time, even those who might have been willing to set aside some of the doctrines of historic Christianity were at the same time unwilling to set aside the morality of historic marriage doctrine. In a destructive shift of views, however, a full wave of secular thinking has now washed over the doctrine of marriage in our society and in the church. Today is found an approach that desires to "present a theological position fully informed by a critical appropriation of the social sciences."[23] Merging two competing bases of authority— theology and social science—has in many quarters resulted in the destruction of the biblical view of marriage.

Many modern writers, even though they write from the perspective of the organized church, have severed the connection between marriage and divine authority, thus opening the door to every conceivable redefinition of marriage: "Single persons and same-sex covenantal unions . . . can be woven into the same theological fabric that includes a theology of marriage."[24] The historic view of marriage has been indicted on several counts, including its insistence that the nuclear family is God's ideal, as well as the possessiveness inherent in traditional marriage. Some even argue that premarital intercourse and cohabitation should be publicly encouraged for engaged couples. Note the radicalism of this language:

> For too long, traditional moralists have been passively allowed to pre-empt often conscientious lifestyles by propagating the unproven assumptions that we cannot love more than one person . . . concurrently; that co-marital or extramarital sex always destroys a marriage; that "good" marriages are totally self-contained and self-restrictive and sufficient.[25]

And now a distinction between "hot sex" and "cool sex":

> Hot sex attitudes (still dominant in our society) are patriarchal, genitally focused, possessive, and performance-obsessed. Cool sex orientation (now making inroads) affirms the equality of the partners, integration rather than competition and conquest, sexual experience as diffused sensuality, an emphasis upon unique personalities and needs, and a tolerance for a pluralism of marital forms.[26]

And it continues:

> [we are not] . . . likely to see the traditional form of marriage retaining its monopolistic sway. I see rather, a future of marital options. . . . There will never be an ultimate or last, in the sense of final, form of

marriage. It will go on changing as the times and the people change and as the demands on it change. *There is no ideal marriage fixed in the nature of things.* . . . We are only now getting used to the idea that any form of marriage is always transitional between an old one and a new one. (emphasis added)[27]

In other words, the very definition of marriage has become *revisable,* placing the historic concept of Christian marriage under a death sentence:

> The possessiveness of an emotional and possibly a genital sort is a major *detriment to the marital relationship.* . . . The nuclear family model has carried with it an image of marriage as an encapsulated sphere, hermetically sealed from relationships of emotional depth with those outside it. . . . If we insist on permanence, exclusivity is harder to enforce; if we insist on exclusivity, permanence may be endangered [italics added]. . . . What is frequently called traditional Christian marriage is itself a product of historical development, and it is not as old as is often believed.[28]

And one final quotation: "In the face of considerable anxiety about change I believe it needs reiteration that no single form of institutional life on earth, marital or otherwise, ought to be considered final. The Sabbath was made for persons and not vice-versa."[29] This last comment is a reminder that these words are written from and for the perspective of the church. For nearly 2,000 years, scholars and teachers associated with the church of Jesus Christ held to a fairly narrow and biblical view of marriage. But no longer. Many voices, not only in our society but also in the church, want to extend marital rights to cohabitants.[30] To do so would be unprecedented in the history of the church.

Writers like these use terms like *covenant* and *bond,* but empty them of the meaning they've held throughout church history. They seem unable to recognize the outrageous mess of using biblical and historical terms to convey concepts that are totally hostile to the established meanings of the terms. A further irony is that a strong secularism influences these writings from people who desire to associate themselves with the church. Many people in our society, including many affiliated with the organized church, have given in to these secular forces, providing a philosophical backdrop for the birth and growth of the modern cohabitation movement. As a result, the traditional and biblical idea of marriage as a sacred, monogamous, lifelong relationship is simply no longer the dominant view.

We can be thankful that many churches, denominations, and Christian organizations continue to hold to a conservative view of marriage, but this conservatism is not found in many other places. The modern and popular conception of marriage has, in fact, made broad inroads. The American Bar Association, in its official publications, states that the definition of marriage and marriage law is in "flux."[31]

Despite this, marriage continues to endure in many quarters. The power of God's ordinance continues to be known. Greeley's comments bear this out:

> [There is an] assumption that our generation has discovered truths that the species never knew before and that will make momentous changes in human relationships undreamed of in the past. Don't hold your breath. Go to a wedding and to a wake—on the same day if you can—and witness the love at both termini of a marriage. See if you really expect marriage to vanish from the earth or to change so that it will no longer be a compelling and compulsive bind together of man and woman. . . . Even if it were possible, as some ideologues seem to think, to strip away all the cultural accretions and begin completely *de novo* with a man and a woman free of all the cultural constraints built up through the ages, would not a new cultural process begin to protect the union which the community and the individuals found so important at the beginning of the species and which they would almost certainly find important again?[32]

Marriage is not going away. And those of us who still accept the idea that marriage descends from God must continue to make the case for the biblical and historic view of marriage covenantalism. If we fail, we'll see continuing devastation across our land. The recent push for the sanctioning of same-sex marriages is another symptom of the destruction of marriage.

What is needed, first and foremost, is a persistent and thorough teaching of marriage as a biblical covenant. Such should begin in the church, for if we don't properly and soundly teach our own, what hope is there for the rest? Further, we need more books the likes of Dahl's older work, *How Can We Keep Christian Marriages from Falling Apart?*—one of the few books I've seen (out of seemingly countless books on marriage available today) that delves into the meaning, significance, and implications of wedding vows.[33] Even most evangelical books on marriage do not go deeply into biblical covenantalism, nor do they stress the meaning of the vows or their connection to the covenant.

There's a laudable emphasis in modern evangelical marriage literature on nurturing marriages and the practical aspects of the marital relationship. For marriages to thrive, however, the seeds of matrimony must be planted in the rich and fertile ground of covenantalism. There seems at last to be a growing emphasis on this latter part of the marital equation. The Puritans nurtured marriages, but the main thrust of their strategy was to expound the nature and obligations of the covenant of marriage. This focus is what gripped our young nation and caused two centuries of family stability.

In premarital classes and at wedding ceremonies, I make it a practice to expound the full nature and meaning of the biblical covenant of marriage. When I do so, expressions of surprise cross the faces of engaged couples and wedding guests. It falls like new rain on cracked and parched soil. There's no lack of emphasis on marriage and family in the evangelical church, but we dare not fail to take people deeply into the theology of marriage. As in the days of the Puritans, a full understanding of the biblical covenant of marriage is needed in the modern church. In the process of reestablishing this understanding, the massive amount of practical and helpful material on marriage now available will be useful. The Halversons, for instance, have much to say after a lifetime of faithful marriage and ministry:

> If we are not careful, "how to" instructions reduce us to consideration of strategies, techniques, and tactics, which go only so far in nurturing any kind of a relationship—least of all the marital union. . . . Often in premarital counseling, I have wished it were possible to communicate adequately to young people beginning life together the incalculable blessings available to couples who honor their marriage covenant no matter how difficult it may seem. . . . For Doris and me, the covenant was simply not negotiable. Everything else was. But it was settled from the beginning that we were entering into an agreement to which God was witness and we saw it an unconditional contract for life. . . . Now, with the perspective of forty years together, we can see how beneficial that constraint was for us. . . . The covenant, taken seriously, provides the *glue* of marriage which holds it together when circumstances or emotions work to destroy the relationship. The covenant is verbalized in the marriage vows, when in the presence of God, loved ones, and friends, a man and woman pledge to receive each other and submit to each other unconditionally for life. The will is the key to this pledge. Where there is the will to honor the covenant, the will to refuse and reject every force that would dishonor it, the will to "cleave" in spite of everything, the very circumstances which might otherwise alienate a couple will be the raw material to strengthen their bond. (emphasis added)[34]

The question now is can the *glue* be applied again in our times? The remaining chapters of this book pursue that goal, particularly for those who have embraced the cohabitation lifestyle.

PART 3

Application

Chapter 9

Christians, Churches, and Cohabiting Couples

A friendly church member asked his pastor about two individuals who were listed in the church's new directory. One was a widow of retirement age, the other a widower, also of retirement age. They were both longtime members of this evangelical church, and no one—including the pastor—had noticed anything special about their relationship. In the new church directory, though, as the friendly member pointed out, both the widow and the widower listed the same address and phone number.

It didn't take the pastor long to process the possibilities suggested by this information. He thanked the questioning church member and pondered his next move. He finally concluded there was little else to do but investigate the situation for himself. His church was too large for him to keep track of the living arrangements of every person under his charge, but he felt a necessity to look into this. The pastor was a good, conscientious man, morally and theologically sound. He felt he had to plunge in, and he did so.

He called the gentleman in question and made a breakfast

appointment to see him, bringing the new directory. They exchanged pleasantries, and during the course of their conversation the pastor took out the directory and showed the man his name and the name of the widow, pointing out the identical addresses and phone numbers. Taking the direct approach, the pastor simply and humbly asked if the man had an explanation for this. The old gentleman chuckled a bit and without any noticeable chagrin said to his much younger pastor, "Oh, yeah, Pastor, I've been meaning to talk to you about that. I guess we better make this thing right."

They'd been living together, in full cohabitation, apart from marriage, for how long the pastor didn't know. *The gentleman chuckled!* The pastor expressed shock that an older couple, whose years in the church added together totaled more than a century, could so casually opt for such an arrangement—and with no apparent concern that their actions might be viewed within the church as something unacceptable. The pastor was left wondering about the condition of his church.

We'd better get used to a weakened notion of marriage, because it's all around us, both in the church and in the wider society. One pastor I know expressed his dismay to a young woman who requested a wedding some years ago. She'd moved away to the "big city" some years before and then desired to come back to her home church for her wedding. So far, so good. But he soon learned that she and her intended were living together (they made no secret of it), had been for several months, and intended to remain so for several more. She was a born-again, baptized member of the church, although she'd been absent for a few years. She said that she just wanted to come back home and be married in her and her family's home church. She made it clear she didn't want any "hassles."

As the premarital process unfolded, it didn't take long to realize that pastor and couple were not going to arrive at a mutual understanding of the proper preparation for Christian marriage. In the end, five families left the church because the pastor "refused" to perform the ceremony. Another family left because the pastor hadn't been "tough enough"! The pastor, though, had never really "refused." Rather, there had been no meeting of the minds between pastor and couple in regard to the crucial elements of the nature and obligations of Christian marriage. The couple was not at all amenable to pastoral guidance and would not do what the pastor requested of them. The scenario that opened this chapter, as well as this preceding scenario, demonstrates a weakened understanding of marriage in the church, as well as a weakened understanding of the moral distinction between marriage and cohabitation.

Consider, too, the lack of understanding among society in general and the many people outside of the church who become "religious" when it's time for a wedding. They've been cohabiting. They show up seeking a blessing for their ceremony, perhaps not comprehending that their present lifestyle is in direct contradiction to Scripture and to the covenant of marriage. Some cohabiting couples, however, begin attending church for other reasons. Maybe the Spirit of God is beginning to do a work in their hearts. Or maybe they're curious. Maybe they're testing the response of the church. Maybe they're completely oblivious to the church's historic view of marriage. Maybe you're reading this book as a Christian deeply concerned about someone you know who's entered a cohabiting relationship or is thinking about it. And you're wondering what to do, what to say, how to respond. Churches, Christians, and pastors will encounter cohabiting couples in our society. The practice is too widespread to avoid, and when we do encounter a cohabiting situation, we'd do well to be prepared. This chapter will be helpful for anyone seeking to counsel with a cohabiting couple or with a person at risk to cohabit.

Ways of Viewing Cohabiting Couples

In my interaction with other Christians, a variety of opinions are held regarding what to do with and say to cohabiting couples. What we do or say depends, of course, on the spiritual condition of the parties in question, our relationship to them, and how much freedom we have to speak candidly. Some of us may have family members in a cohabiting relationship, some of us may have children on the verge of it, some of us may see it all around us in our work places. Pastors will encounter cohabiting couples in the same way that others do, as well as through the normal course of pastoral work. What should we do? What should we say?

Make It Right!

Some seem to think we ought to urge cohabiting couples just to make things right. That is, we should press them to get married as soon as possible. Marriage is, after all, a God-given right and reflects God's will for humanity. So let's just be nice to cohabiting couples, keep an open relationship with them, avoid being judgmental, but when we have the chance, urge them to marry. This approach might be especially important for those couples who seem to have chosen cohabitation as a long-term alternative to marriage.

Tolerance

This is a word everyone likes today. So some suggest that Christians keep quiet about the cohabitation that occurs in our circles of friends and families. Pastors also should be accepting—live and let live. When it comes to cohabiters, let God do His work in their hearts in His own time. Cohabitation is, after all, widely accepted today, and we're not able, really, to do anything about that. So we should avoid outward moral judgments and attempts at correction. Simply try to be friendly and accepting toward all, keep the peace and see what happens down the road.

Focus on the Relationship

This point of view urges that we suspend any moral judgments and just talk about what it means and what it takes to have a long-term, loving relationship. If we can help cohabiting couples grow in their understanding of what commitment is, what sacrifice is, what love is, they'll eventually move in the right direction. This approach is pragmatic, and those holding it seem to want, above all, the relationship to last. That's the higher good, and it's hoped that marriage will result if the relationship becomes stable.

All of these views avoid the harsher edge of moral judgment and stop short of challenging cohabiting couples with the full reality of what God has said in His Word. No corrective steps are suggested in the above views, and for that reason they provide inadequate solutions. I was talking with a church leader about this, stressing my own strong feelings about trying to correct cohabiting couples. This leader said to me, "I don't look at it that way. That's too narrow. I just accept them and hope for the best." I don't agree. I think we have to take a more active posture and at least seek an opportunity to share God's better plan for couples.

The Corrective View

There isn't a lot of help available on the subject of counseling with cohabiting couples. I've studied all the premarital counseling guides I could find that have been written and published over the last fifty years. Not even more recent ones specifically address cohabiting couples. I've also examined evangelical books on marriage and marital preparation. Despite the publication of books by the metric ton on this subject, almost nothing in depth can be found in them about cohabitation. I don't know of any single book published in America that specifically addresses the subject of cohabitation from an evangelical point of view. This despite our talking about it and encountering the lifestyle on a daily basis. Thus, when it comes to evangelicals counseling with cohabiting couples, this volume appears to be one of the few to offer suggestions.

Shouldn't we at least try to correct couples who are cohabiting, for their own sakes if for nothing else? We might be able to help someone or help a couple find God's path, which will put their relationship on much more stable footing. The other, higher reason to offer correction is the glory of God. The prayer of Jesus was that God's will might be done on earth as it is in heaven. God has a plan for marriage, and it cannot please Him when it's casually tossed aside. I encourage you, then, to look for an opportunity to share your thoughts with your cohabiting friend, neighbor, or relative. Surely we would do the same thing for a married friend who was not fulfilling the God-given obligations of Scripture regarding marriage. Would we just tolerate or accept a friend or relative pursuing and maintaining an adulterous relationship? I don't think so! Pastors especially, as the guardians of God's Word in the church, should not shrink back from challenging and correcting cohabiting couples. The suggestions below offer an approach.

Give an Explanation of What the Bible Teaches

Give a firm and clear explanation of the Bible's teaching on marriage and cohabitation. Every couple, whatever their spiritual background, deserves to hear this. Remember, many people in our society are biblically illiterate—they do not at all grasp what God has said about life and living. What good can be gained by holding back this information? A cohabiting couple needs to hear that their choice of relationship does not fulfill God's plan, desire, or will. Call cohabitation sinful—how can a sinner be saved unless that person learns that he or she is a sinner? Display some conviction when you do this. Do it in love, but don't back down. Your cohabiting friend should realize that what you say is not based in your own opinions, but in God's

Word. You also may have an opportunity to share the gospel, which is the deeper need of many in a cohabiting relationship. Certainly you may run the risk of straining the relationship. So it's wise to say what you say with a measure of tact, good judgment, and kindness. You want to leave an open and intact relationship when you're finished.

Maintain a Gracious Manner

If you've been saved by the grace of God and are living under God's daily forgiveness, then maintaining grace shouldn't require a lot of effort. Humbled by grace and living in the broken inadequacy of our own lives, we should be able to correct people without a harsh, condemning spirit. You, then, want to be firm and clear about what God's Word says, but in a way that gives a high priority to demonstrating love to the person you're correcting. We want to help people find their way, ultimately, to God's grace. Most couples, whether cohabiting or married, desperately want to succeed in their relationship. Thus, make it clear that you want this also. I often say to couples, "I'm sharing this with you for two reasons; one is I care about God and His will and I also care about you and your life." Most people sense I'm not attempting to crush them but to lift them to something higher. So do what you can to draw others into your trust and then tell them the truth as graciously as you can.

Lay Out the Arguments

Lay out the best arguments against cohabitation and the best arguments for marriage. Refer to the list below:

- *Breakups.* Share with cohabiters that most cohabiting relationships don't last. Only 10 or 15 percent of cohabiting relationships survive ten years, even if marriage comes at some point. Breakups are especially likely for those who enter the cohabiting relationship with little clarity about where the relationship is going. Breaking up takes only one partner who says, "That's it." Such is the nature of the relationship.

- *Baggage.* If a breakup does occur, much baggage will be carried into the next relationship. Will one or both partners go on to make the same mistakes again? When will the serial cohabitation stop? Present to them the reality of becoming a "serial cohabiter." After a breakup it might become even more difficult to have a long-term relationship because of issues of trust, commitment, and hurt. These burdens are a hazard of the cohabitation lifestyle.

- *Divorce.* For those who go on to marry their cohabiting partner, statistics show that about one-third of them will be divorced within two years. After ten years, that number balloons to about two-thirds. Many go into a cohabiting relationship, hoping it will help them avoid divorce. Actually, it helps them *on to* divorce. The better path is to maintain purity prior to marriage and get premarital counseling upon entering marriage.

- *Unfaithfulness.* Research shows that cohabiting couples have a greater propensity to be sexually unfaithful to one another, even after a marriage takes place. People willing to cohabit seem to have a weaker moral code. Unfaithfulness can be devastating and can strike the blow that ends the relationship.

- *Commitment.* Share with them that when they enter a cohabiting relationship, no true commitment is made. Either party can leave at any time, that being the nature of the agreement. Each partner may find himself or herself constantly wondering if the other party will leave. Meanwhile, months and years pass by and the couple is no closer to the security of marriage.

- *Common goals.* Does each half of the couple know for sure that his or her partner has the same understanding of the relationship? Often men are looking for a convenient sex partner and women are looking for a future marriage partner, a reality that should be pointed out, particularly to women. Thus, the potential that someone will get used in a cohabiting relationship is strong.

- *Legalities.* Cohabiting couples have few legal rights regarding the person with whom they cohabit. Each may not even be able to sign documents admitting their partner to the hospital. Dilemmas arise, too, over any property purchased together. All manner of deficiencies and quagmires can result from these relationships.
- *Selfishness.* The practice of cohabitation is inherently selfish. Cohabiting individuals want something from their partners but they're unwilling to give much in return. Cohabitation is all about what one can get, without giving. Do we really think that relationships based on such attitudes will succeed?
- *History.* Cohabitation is a novelty in our society. The results of the modern experiment with this lifestyle are just now being studied, and they're not promising. Marriage, however, has worked well in the past and works today in most places in the world. Cohabitation has not proved itself as an effective, stable, productive institution.
- *Future.* Plans for the future have to be put on hold during a cohabiting relationship. Cohabitants do not store up for retirement together, because they don't know if they'll still be together. Nor do cohabitants often name one another as beneficiaries on life insurance policies. Cohabitation short-circuits many practices that often have long-term benefits for a couple.
- *Family and friends.* Cohabitants should realize that their lifestyle may be deeply troubling to others. Family and friends, although not saying much, may, however, be very upset, negatively impacting relationships for years. As stated above, cohabitation is often a selfish lifestyle choice (people think of themselves and not their friends and families), and selfishness almost always damages relationships. Cohabiting, too, can affect one's future

children. What will be said to children about the period of
cohabitation? It should be pointed out, especially to younger
people, that they may one day be embarrassed about their
cohabiting.

- *God and church.* Perhaps the greatest evil of the cohabiting
  lifestyle is that it creates distance from God and His church. A
  moral darkening comes with all sexual sin. Share with the
  couple what Hebrews 13:4 says. The church, too, is committed to nurturing relationships and giving guidance on the most
  important decisions of life. Since most cohabitants exit the
  church, cohabiting will remove this positive influence from
  their lives.

In contrast to the above negative elements of cohabitation, marriage provides many positives. In marriage, couples make a solid,
mutually understood commitment, reaching a meeting of the minds
as to what the future holds, and early on investing in the long-term
dimensions of the relationship. Sexual faithfulness is strengthened by
marriage, and remaining in or returning to the church is easier with a
clear conscience before God. Friends and family normally rejoice, and
couples won't have to look forward to a day when they must make
painful revelations to their children. Couples experience the legal protections of marriage, and the relationship has a much greater chance
of achieving stability. Studies show that marriage is more likely to
produce feelings of happiness and satisfaction as couples learn to give
and not to focus so much on themselves. Marriage, too, helps the
process of building a legacy. Given all of these benefits, why would
anyone choose to cohabit?

When considering the situation of cohabiters, I think of my grandmother. Her mother died in childbirth when Grandmother was around
eighteen years old, leaving several small children. As the oldest, my
grandmother stayed at home and helped her father raise her younger
brothers and sisters until the last one was grown. Sacrificing for others,

Grandmother didn't get married until many years later. All of her life she manifested a self-forgetting commitment to others, yet she attended college, become a teacher, and taught me to read before I went to school. My mother had those same qualities of giving to others. Although I didn't realize it at the time, looking back I realize the cocoon of comfort and protection my mother put around me every day of my life as I grew up. What, though, if my grandmother had gone out and sought her own pleasures in her twenties, instead of being devoted to her family? What if she'd sworn off marriage like so many do today? What if my mother hadn't been marked by a person like my grandmother? How would my life have been different? Relationships are not just about personal happiness and selfish concerns, they also create a legacy and a heritage. Cohabiting couples would thus do well to think about the long-term impact of what they're doing.

One couple came to me to talk about their daughter, who wanted to get married. They were deeply concerned about her age and the age of her intended—both only nineteen. The young couple had not yet finished their education and had only part-time jobs. What would they live on? I calmed the worried parents as best I could and said, "Let me meet with them and see what I can do."

I did meet with them—twice as a matter of fact, both times for the better part of two hours. And guess what? They were two of the most prepared people for marriage I'd ever counseled. They were mature, astute, stable, and in love. They had a plan and had thought through most of the practicalities of starting their life together. It was a great blessing talking with them, and I wish I could bottle what they had going on in their lives. A lot of people could use it.

That this young couple was so prepared was not all that surprising. They were both from strong, stable Christian homes, and were exemplary young people who had a history of involvement in their churches. Later, I informed their parents that they were victims of their own success, raising two great kids. I told them I had no qualms about the couple getting married. They did get married soon after, and I had the privilege of performing the ceremony. They've gone on to have a wonderful marriage.

Yes, the youth of a couple can be a concern when they're considering marriage. But it's not the most important concern. If, in the full blossom of youth, couples marry for all the right reasons and begin building a life together early, that life will eventually become a legacy for others. This is the way God intended it to be. Too many people, on the other hand, are waiting much too long to get married. Our youth culture is so fearful of commitment that they're postponing marriage on average until the late twenties. Doing so creates much more temptation for sexual involvement and cohabitation. If we as pastors, advisors, and friends could help people shed the fear of marriage, our whole society would be more stable and have a more promising future. How, though, can we do that? We can teach young people what it means to make a covenant of marriage and encourage them to find someone who shares the same view. They can then go on to form their own covenants of marriage and enter into unbreakable unions for life, under God's watchful eye. When a couple has that, they have what they need to build a life and a legacy.

Suggest Corrective Steps

Every person's cohabiting situation is a little different, so we must tailor our remarks to suit the situation. When talking with a young college student, for example, after covering the other points above, we might suggest something like the following: "You can see that what you're doing is wrong and will be hazardous for your future. Why not have a talk with your partner and reestablish a more conventional dating relationship?" When counseling with a cohabiting couple with previous marriages and children in the home, we might suggest, "For the sake of your children and the stability of their home and your relationship, you need to get some good counseling and begin to move toward marriage." To a young professional who hasn't given much thought to the future, we might say, "There's every likelihood that this is going to end up badly for you. Then what? I strongly encourage you to rethink the choices you've made." To a couple heading toward marriage who intends to move in together for pragmatic reasons, we might share how they can put their relationship on a more exciting and stable plane by waiting until after their wedding to live together and become sexually intimate. In other words, we should consider each couple or individual's situation and simply counsel them sensibly, pointing out the best way to get from their immoral and harmful choice to a more godly and healthy lifestyle.

Armed with all of these arguments and practical suggestions, many of us will likely have opportunities to teach others about God's plan for marriage and, as well, His plan for salvation. Thus, we can be used of God to help them turn toward His way, as the Spirit of grace works in their hearts. We might not succeed with everyone. We might not succeed with anyone! But we can know, at the end of the day, that we've been about God's work. And on those days when God gives us a victory, however small, we will rejoice greatly.

A friend, "Bill," told me about a younger man, "Johnny," with whom he'd worked for a few years. Bill and Johnny were fairly close friends, and through some casual comments Bill suspected that Johnny had moved in with his girlfriend, although he hadn't come right out and said so. Bill worked up the nerve to ask Johnny about it. "Are you living with Sheryl now?" he asked. "How come you're doing that?" Johnny seemed a little embarrassed and gave a halting answer that they were just doing so to "save money" and were not involved sexually. Bill challenged him and said, "If I pulled ten people off the street right now and told them about your living together but not having sex, how many would believe it?" Johnny answered, "Probably none," and then he admitted that they were involved sexually. Bill helped the young man see that if he was lying about his relationship with his girlfriend—feeling guilty day after day, not being straight even with his friends—then living together probably wasn't a good idea. Bill and Johnny talked at length, and the young man later that same day had a long talk with his girlfriend. They decided it would be better to wait for marriage to live together, and they corrected their living situation.

What might happen if a couple decides to rectify their cohabiting? First, from a moral standpoint, doing so makes their relationship right with God. The darkening power of sexual sin will begin to lift and the conscience of each will become more tender toward God. Second, they may begin to think of what God wants rather than just what they want. Such a powerful change in attitude will greatly help them should they go on to marry. Third, it helps them have a more serious view of marriage and will most likely help prevent a future marital disruption. Fourth, it may help the couple to reacquire sexual purity in their relationship. Once this happens, they'll begin to build their relationship upon friendship and companionship rather than upon sex. Fifth, it might help them look forward to marriage with a positive mindset. Their wedding day and honeymoon will once again be a special gift, and they'll feel freedom, rather than bondage, when they marry.

Firm and gracious counsel—with a suggestion of how to take corrective steps—might work from time to time, depending, of course, upon the depth of one's relationship with the couples—or to one of the partners—and their openness to receiving counsel. Not every cohabiting person or couple will be obliging toward those who try to counsel them, nor may the person or couples seriously consider such counsel. But some might. And what a good work we will have done if this happens! Marriage is such a better way, and we can have a part in helping a person or a couple to reclaim this gift of God.

On Monday, July 10, 1995, the *Dallas Morning News* carried an article titled, "Post-wedding bliss: Now it's pizza, not sex." The thrust of the article was that, given the common acceptance of premarital sex and cohabitation, the fabled wedding night experience was disappearing. Sex has lost its importance as a key part in the wedding experience, because the common pattern today is to have sex first, then move in together, and then, if all goes well, get married.

The article cited one couple's wedding night experience. The couple indicated that, on their wedding night, sex was the last thing on their minds. They arrived at their hotel hungry and tired after an elaborate wedding, a dinner, and several hours of dancing at their reception. So when they got to their beautiful hotel suite, they simply ordered pizza, watched a movie, and fell asleep. No sex. So much for the blushing bride and the stumbling groom. So much for the bliss of marital discovery.

Such "honeymooners"—all too common today—have already established sexual familiarity long before the wedding day. This partly explains new wedding traditions I've observed such as lengthy, exhausting wedding day activities and morning-after present opening parties with family and friends in attendance. I find it odd, however, when a couple doesn't crave to be alone and together after their wedding. Rather, the aforementioned practices seem to signal a diminished desire for intimacy on the part of the couple. The wedding events, with the parties and prizes, have supplanted the exciting union and physical bonding of the bride and groom. I don't think this is how God meant it to be.

The special coming together of a man and woman under vow and divine presence has been sacrificed on the altar of premarital sex and cohabitation. The joy of marital sex, in all its blessed discoveries, has been cheapened. If, then, God puts us as counselors and friends in a place where we can help someone recover what's been lost, we ought to give it our best and most earnest effort. Pray hard, speak graciously, and tell the couple what God has said in His Word. Then, if there's an opening to do so, suggest how they can amend their decision and move toward God's ideal.

Chapter 10

Pastoral Counseling
with Cohabiting Couples

Two Key Principles

A few years ago, an Anglican vicar from Gloucester, England, urged his fellow pastors to adopt a new policy. His aim was to deal with the large numbers of cohabiting couples in England, and his solution was to suspend the normal fees the church charges for weddings in the hope that unmarried couples could be lured to the altar and away from cohabiting. He further urged that all usual participants in weddings, such as organists and musicians, forego their honorariums. Higher officials in the Anglican church were unimpressed by the proposal. The Church of England would stand to lose more than the equivalent of thirty million dollars per year if fees were no longer charged for weddings. Apparently, the vicar's proposal was considered a bad idea.[1]

A certain desperation might easily overtake pastors in regard to cohabiting couples. Pastors often sense their marginalization in a society that's forsaken God's teaching on marriage. But it's a lamentable state of affairs when pastors are tempted to take large steps toward the secular culture when what really needs to happen is for the secular culture to take large steps toward God. And if pastors take a strong and uncompromising stand on the morality of cohabitation, it can end badly for them. A few years ago, a remarkable example of a modern-day pastoral dilemma found its way into American popular culture. It began with a letter to "Dear Abby." A woman wrote, stating that she had an issue that Abby, the icon of popular advice, had never before addressed: a clergyman who would not officiate the wedding of a couple who was "living together" prior to the nuptials. The writer of the letter was the mother of the denied bride-to-be.

Her daughter had lived with her fiancé a few months before the wedding, and when the minister discovered it, he refused to participate in the wedding. He had moral objections. Surprisingly, the mother took the minister's side, stating that she was glad that some churches were still upholding standards and teaching respect for marriage. The couple in question was chagrined and angry but made other arrangements for their wedding. Initially, Abby's comments supported the mother and the clergyman's stand.

Later in the year, however, Abby returned to the subject on not less than three occasions because of the volume of mail she received concerning this letter and her initial response. In later columns she began to backtrack from her previous support of the clergyman, admitting that she became more "enlightened" as she read the subsequent mail. The mail writers expressed outrage and dismay at the mother and the clergyman, who were both roundly condemned. These sentiments were expressed with surprising conviction and consistency. Not only were the mother and the pastor held to be completely out of touch, but also intolerant and self-righteous.

Abby ultimately changed her mind and was led to agree with the lecturing writers, who proclaimed that the church is supposed to be forgiving. Moreover, they pointed out what was to them an obvious truth: couples are wise to live together before marriage (an example of the conventional wisdom prevailing in the popular mind well into the 1990s). The letter writers noted that this couple was obviously sufficiently "committed," even though not married. The overwhelming conclusion was that the clergyman was totally wrong.

This discussion in a popular advice column demonstrates that when it comes to the meaning and sacredness of marriage, there's a wide gap between today's popular culture and biblically informed pastors. The "Abby" drama mirrors the common experiences of many pastors as they interact with American culture, which perceives "living together" (or cohabitation) as a nonobjectionable alternative or preliminary to marriage. Since pastors still perform the overwhelming majority of marriage ceremonies, and since many cohabitants do go on to marry, it's a certainty that pastors and churches will encounter cohabiting couples. Many cohabiters, too, are led to attend church long before they consider approaching a pastor concerning a wedding.

What's a pastor to do? There are, of course, nuances and shades of gray in dealing with the host of couples who may be living together apart from marriage, and it's clear that not all pastors agree on the issue of cohabitation, let alone agree on every individual case. But a lengthy study of cohabitation, as well as extensive conversations with pastors, has led to the development of some guidelines. They are also based upon what the Bible says about marriage. Given that marriage is declared as a sacred covenant, there is little choice but to teach, promote, and enforce this understanding with those who place themselves under our charge.

It won't always be easy to apply the biblical doctrine of marriage to couples who may not have the faintest clue concerning the sacred nature of God's ordinance. Many couples seek a wedding from a pastor as casually as they would seek a plumber to fix a leaky pipe. They want a ceremony without being inconvenienced, so pastors may not be able to avoid scenarios like that described in "Dear Abby." They should, however, be prepared to deal with cohabiting couples in a knowledgeable, relevant, biblical, and constructive fashion.

Clarifying the Issues

What should a pastor do with a cohabiting couple? I've been asking pastors that question for many years, and have come to recognize some distinctions at the outset, particularly in how and why a pastor encounters a cohabiting couple. First, a pastor may meet a cohabiting couple who are casually attending that pastor's church. Such a couple might be genuinely led of the Spirit as God draws them to faith, or they might be just checking things out. The church, after all, invites sinners to experience the grace of God and learn what it is to come into a saving relationship with Christ. Thus, a pastor should welcome such a couple to worship or to Bible study. Most pastors would likely agree that there's no need for immediate and drastic action simply because people in a sinful lifestyle have come to visit and attend church services. Let them come, and then see what God does in their hearts as they hear the truth and see the love of Christ in the congregation.

Many pastors would obviously feel differently if one or both of the cohabitants were professing believers, particularly if he or she were a church member. As noted earlier, the Bible says that this kind of sin is not to be named as among us. Consequently, pastors should in such cases be inclined, as the apostle Paul taught, to lead their churches through a process of restorative discipline. The goal is, of course, correction and restoration, which can be a difficult process. But surely it's in the long-term interests of the church and the parties involved to do so. Many years ago a tiny church in a rural area was faced with a thirty-something divorced woman—a born-again baptized member of the church—who moved in with a man. The pastor struggled to get his little flock to adopt a posture of loving correction and discipline. Rural ties run deep and this woman was well liked and a relative of several people in the church. After months of persuasion and numerous fruitless exhortations to the woman in question, they at last publicly disciplined her. It took some years, but the woman finally repented, corrected her lifestyle, and later thanked the pastor and members for what they'd done. This process can work, and regardless of whether the immediate results are positive or not, it's the right and biblical thing to do.

What if a cohabiting couple desires a pastor to perform their wedding? This question has become crucial in modern pastoral work. Should the pastor refuse on the basis of the clear immorality of the cohabiting lifestyle? Should the pastor urge them to "make it right" as soon as possible? Can every situation be resolved the same way? Does it change anything if children are part of the equation? What if there's newfound faith in Christ on the part of the couple? Sometimes, when a couple approaches the church for a wedding, it represents the first time in a long time that they've sought help, counsel, or anything from the church. That the cohabiting couple has, indeed, approached the pastor presents a ministry opportunity for the pastor in terms of evangelism, teaching, guidance, and correction. Whatever a pastor decides to do, it must be both biblically defensible and helpful in a practical way. Theological underpinnings cannot be overlooked, nor can the typical consequences of modern cohabitation.

It would be in order, then, to survey some of the issues involved in resolving these questions. First, pastors do have different standards and guidelines regarding those whom they wed. Many evangelical pastors require evidence of saving faith in Christ on the part of the couple before agreeing to perform a wedding. Some will marry a couple who has not yet come to faith, hoping to build bridges. Most will not marry a believer to a nonbeliever, given the injunctions of Scripture on this point. So this matter of faith on the part of a couple might limit some pastors when they consider marrying a cohabiting couple. In our church it's become next to impossible to marry people in our community who don't make our church their church home. There are simply too many requests. Thus, we can only agree to marry members and regular attendees. So pragmatics can be a concern in the "Who do we marry?" question.

What, though, should we do with cohabiting couples who want

the pastor to perform their wedding ceremony? Many pastors have struggled to find an acceptable policy on this question and many others have no policy at all. Some pastors give an absolute *no* to all cohabiting couples, refusing in the initial interview, if not before. Most pastors point out, however, that it's wise to meet with any couple who desires a wedding even if the answer is likely to be "no." Questions can be structured so that the couple ultimately decides whether they'll be married in the pastor's church. The pastor can say something like, "Here are our guidelines and rules. Are you interested in doing it this way?" We've seen some fruit in our own church's ministry in initial interviews, as God sends us people who, although involved in a sinful relationship, are ready to listen and respond to the gospel.

A common approach among some pastors will be to marry cohabiting couples but only with corrective action and thorough premarital counseling. The corrective action usually involves reestablishing separate households and a recommitment to sexual purity. The counseling often includes some guidance on how to correct the potential harm the willingness to cohabit may have done to their relationship and their understanding of marriage.

Some pastors treat cohabiting couples like any other couple and provide merely standard premarital counseling. No corrective action is initiated and the cohabiting state is glossed over. Such an approach may not, however, fully reveal the underlying problems in the attitudes and values of the cohabitants. Certainly, the premarital counseling can address these matters, but will the moral and attitudinal deficiencies be successfully overcome when the couple takes no *action?* Plus another moral issue begs the question: In taking this approach does the pastor, in his role as a representative of the Lord's church, accept blatant sin?

Some pastors will marry cohabitants, but only outside of the church—and the sooner the better. These pastors, looking at the positive side, feel that a marriage at least "makes things right," and it may seem like the best solution for certain cohabiting couples. In such situations, pastors often provide premarital or postmarital counseling. On the negative side, one has to wonder about the stability of the subsequent union, given the possible attitudes and values of the couple. Making the situation "right" is not the same as embracing a full biblical covenant of marriage.

Some pastors perform weddings, feeling that the wedding and the marriage are the moral responsibility of the couple, not the pastor. Such pastors see themselves as servants to the couples (and to the state), empowered to marry couples. Marriage is, after all, a God-given right, so this thinking goes, not restricted to believers or to those who are morally pure. Others object to this approach, pointing to the biblical and historic calling of pastors to seek amendment in the lives they touch. Can pastors merely see themselves as agents of the state? Or are they first and foremost agents of Jesus Christ, charged with proclaiming God's message that "all men everywhere repent" (Acts 17:30)?

Many pastors use a case-by-case approach. Some do so because they haven't yet thought through how to handle cohabiters; others may see genuine distinctions between the cohabiting couples they minister to. Pastors may judge each case on certain merits such as sincerity, repercussions in the church, and the families involved. The pastor taking this approach can run the risk of looking and being inconsistent, and may also overlook the unique needs of cohabiting couples in terms of premarital preparation.

From my discussions with pastors, it's clear that many are concerned with the moral condition of cohabiters. The pastors are seeking to lead people to a saving relationship with Christ, seeking to amend lives, and seeking to prepare couples for marriage. When it comes to cohabiting couples, most evangelical pastors seem to use a combination of correction and counseling. They may exercise some flexibility within their individual policies, recognizing that not all cohabiting couples are "created equal." But the most common approach reflects most evangelical pastors' view that cohabitation is not only a risky choice in view of the future stability of the marriage, but also as an immoral practice and a defiance of God's ordinance of marriage.

The issue of cohabitation certainly gives pastors much to ponder. Thus, offered below is a discussion of two broad suggestions, followed in the next chapter by more specific suggestions for pastors who encounter cohabiting couples.

Principle Number One: Be Open to God's Leading

One pastor reported on a friendship he struck up with a neighborhood couple who was cohabiting. He invited them to church numerous times, and finally they did come, with their two children. After attending church a few weeks, they fell under deep conviction of their need of Christ and were gloriously saved. And I mean saved. They ran out and bought Bibles and quickly sought to be baptized. And then, yes, it did occur to them that they ought to be married, and so they got married, too. Such wonderful outcomes can occur—cohabiting couples are part of the mission field to which God sends us.

Perhaps, then, it's best to assume that when a cohabiting couple attends one of our churches or approaches a pastor for a wedding, they are doing so in response to a leading of the Spirit. Thus, the pastor *must* keep the leading of the Spirit in view. It could be that couples are presenting themselves for entirely different reasons and, if so, time will usually tell. But the wiser course for a pastor surely is to be open to the spiritual needs of cohabiting couples. Thus, the following approach is suggested.

Pastors Should Be Willing to Meet with Cohabiting Couples

Given that cohabitation is sexual sin and that it is underlain by a rejection of marriage, pastors may have difficulty overcoming their strong feelings about what a cohabiting couple is doing. These feelings should not, however, foreclose at least a friendly meeting at which moral matters can be discussed. In such a meeting, pastors have every liberty to express their views in a loving and straightforward manner. And God may use that meeting to initiate repentance on the part of the couple.

Without making any promises to couples, pastors can probe their lifestyle attitudes, perhaps opening an opportunity to share the gospel and/or the biblical teaching on marriage. Whatever specific policies pastors may have for cohabiting couples, it seems clear they should at least give the couple access to moral and spiritual guidance. If such guidance is spurned and resisted, at least the pastor has tried. If such a couple responds to guidance, the pastor could be on the way to participating in a glorious spiritual victory. It seems best, then, to meet with such couples and see what God will do in their hearts.

Pastors Should Discern the Moral and Spiritual Condition of Cohabiting Couples

I have no qualms about making a thorough assessment of a cohabiting couple's background, relationship, and present intentions. Why are they cohabiting? How did it start? What kind of moral background do they have? Where are they now spiritually? Are they seeking to be married now? Why? How does the man look at the relationship? The woman? Why are they in church talking to a pastor?

This approach requires patient listening but may guide the pastor into a clear understanding of the mind-set of the couple. One time I was probing a very young cohabiting couple in this manner, and the more I probed the more sound and strong their attitude seemed to be concerning the proper view of marriage. Moreover, the young man professed to have come to faith in Christ just a few months earlier, and the young woman went on to make a profession of faith in that very first interview. At one point I couldn't help but ask, "If you believe all this, why in the world did you ever move in together?"

They looked dumbfounded, shrugged their shoulders, looked at one another, and said very little. They had no compelling reason or any clear explanation. They had, in fact, the same look on their faces that my youngest child has when she does something she's not supposed to do, but has no explanation for it. This couple proved to defy some of the generalizations that are made about cohabiting couples. They are still married today, many years later. The point is, in probing, pastors learn in what direction their counsel needs to go.

Pastors Should Be Ready to Persuasively Present the Pitfalls of the Cohabiting Lifestyle

The results of social research and the statistics presented in this book and in other sources are sufficient to cause cohabiting couples to reflect deeply on the wisdom of what they're doing. Thus, pastors should make it a point to present this kind of information. Younger couples, college and high school students, and young singles should be a target of this information as well. The statistics bear out that any couple who cohabits puts the future stability of their relationship in peril, and their risk of splitting up or having an unhappy marriage and divorcing is very high.

Pastors Must Not Alter or Diminish the Biblical Evaluation of Cohabitation as a Form of Sexual Sin

To gloss over the state of sin is unthinkable. Nor should any pastor apologize for starting with the morality of the Bible, which reflects God's will and wisdom. How can we *not* present it? If someone is well outside the revealed will of God, it's not helpful to keep silent about it. Certainly pastors can show God's leading in love and kindness but the secular mind needs to be exposed to the biblical mind. Remember, many cohabiting couples do possess some moral foundation, however damaged or limited it might be. And given the terrible consequences likely to ensue when couples ignore God's wisdom on marriage, pastors should be doubly careful to outline all the Bible says about cohabitation from the standpoint of morality and marriage.

So, first, pastors should be open to meeting with cohabiting couples with a view toward seeing how God might work in their hearts as they receive the truth. Second, pastors should present God's truth to them in love, holding nothing back. They need to understand what God has said about marriage and sexual sin.

Principle Number Two: Have a Clear Policy

The second broad suggestion on this matter is that pastors think through and develop a policy for cohabiting couples. Having such a policy in place will help pastors, first of all, prepare for the inevitability of couples seeking them out. The policy, too, will provide some understanding and consistency within the church.

Those pastors who have policies on cohabiting couples feel that they are much more effective in the difficult pastoral dilemmas that cohabiting couples can create. Some pastors have a policy but it has not been very well communicated to the leadership of the church or to the congregation. Such doesn't seem wise. It's best if the policy is in written form and has been part of leadership discussions. That way, it can further serve an educational purpose in the church. It can be posted on a bulletin board, published in a church newsletter, handed out to young people, taught in a college and singles ministry, and issued to whoever has a question about it.

With a written policy in place, it's made clear that any action taken in regard to a cohabiting couple extends not from personal opinion, but from the deep conviction of the pastor and church leadership. Consistency in the implementation of such a policy is vital. One church member told me about a young man in our congregation who was thinking about moving in with his girlfriend. The member said to him, "Do you realize that there's a written policy against that in our church?" It was enough to dissuade the young man from following through. Pastors can also find themselves being tempted to compromise their convictions when the policy is not down in black and white.

It may be that a policy can be written with some flexibility given the different sorts of couples who might cohabit. But any policy should delineate the corrective steps that will be expected from those who are in a cohabiting relationship. Such specific steps, presented as church policy, will provide pastors with a little "backbone" as they meet with couples. It also suggests to the couple that they've done something very wrong and haven't taken the proper steps in preparing for marriage. And surely it pleases God that we so honor His plan and will that we put down clearly on paper that we expect people to obey Him in the crucial area of forming a new bond of marriage. But more on this in the next chapter.

These two broad suggestions lay a foundation for sound pastoral work. We remain open to people, yet determined to have people obey God. Did Moses, Paul, or the Lord Jesus do any differently? Certainly we can build upon this foundation, but without it, we miss much of what is fundamental in ministering to people in today's world.

Some years ago I read about Haron and Lola Howell, who had been married sixty-three years.[2] They were an Iowa farm couple who refused Clint Eastwood's request to use their farmhouse for scenes in the film *The Bridges of Madison County*. They objected that the plot of the movie concerned an adulterous relationship. Mrs. Howell said, "We have four children, twelve grandchildren, and fifteen great-grandchildren, and they all come here a lot. They would think, 'Yeah, Grandma's just like everybody else.'" They simply did not want to be party to the values represented by the film. Clint Eastwood had to go elsewhere.

The stand taken by the Howells demonstrates that, in regard to marriage and sexuality, a stronger moral foundation once existed in this nation. That foundation will continue to crumble in today's moral climate, even within the church. The question is, can it be restored?

Sound pastoral work must be part of the effort to do so. It is incumbent upon pastors to lead the effort to restore a proper approach to marriage in our society and churches.

So pastors should be open to meeting with people in cohabiting relationships—that is gospel work. But pastors also should remember that they must speak from God's Word in every pastoral opportunity, including those times they meet with cohabiting couples or with an individual cohabitant. A well thought-through, written policy reflecting the teaching of God's Word will stand a pastor in good stead for such an occasion.

These two broad principles form the foundation of proper pastoral work with cohabiting couples. I make no prognostications as to success when these principles are applied in pastoral work. I do submit, however, that they reflect sound pastoral work in view of the biblical and historic calling of pastoral ministry. Implementation of these principles will evidence biblical fidelity, love for people, serious thought, and pastoral integrity. And these are the elements of what pastoral work should be.

Chapter 11

Pastoral Counseling with Cohabiting Couples

Specific Guidelines

One pastor, ministering in a small town, reacted with some shock in an initial premarital counseling appointment. The couple gave him the same address, and it was the first time he'd encountered this situation. Upon clarifying that they were, in fact, cohabiting, he, thinking fast, informed them that he didn't think he'd be able to perform their wedding. "Maybe," he said, "if you agree to live apart until the wedding, I can think about it." The couple was offended and angry. One of the partners' parents included a man who was a deacon in the church. In a subsequent phone conversation, the deacon was clearly upset with how the pastor had handled the situation. Several meetings were held with the deacon, his wife, the couple, and other church leaders. The pastor tried to explain his convictions, but the family pointed to others who'd been married over the years in the church, including some brides who'd been pregnant at the time of their wedding. Later, the couple refused to engage in any premarital counseling with the pastor, yet the family insisted that the wedding go forward. In the end, the pastor consented to perform the ceremony, but the relationship between the couple and him remained strained, and the wedding was not very pleasant. The relationship between the pastor and the deacon's family never completely healed.

Specific Guidelines

Could this outcome have been avoided if the pastor and the church had in place a clear, written policy regarding cohabiting couples? This pastor thought so, later remarking that as a result of this difficult situation "a new personal premarital policy" has made for a stronger premarital counseling ministry. He learned that it was best to "hit it hard up front rather than backpeddling later on." But the point remains that many pastors have experienced considerable strife because of a cohabiting situation that emerges in their church.

Almost all the pastors I talk to indicate that they've been approached by cohabiting couples for a wedding. Cohabitation is not an abstract phenomenon written about in sociological journals; it's a reality intersecting the lives of Christians, churches, and pastors no matter the size or location of a church. Small-town pastors are surrounded by cohabiting couples. Some suburban pastors are more insulated from it. Other large suburban churches encounter cohabiters all the time. One pastor from a small-town ministry remarked that he received a good number of wedding requests from his community, including cohabiting couples, simply because his church has lower fees for a wedding than any of the other churches in the area! Clearly, pastors are interacting with cohabiting couples.

Any pastor who ministers for twenty years and encounters two cohabiting couples per year will interact with forty over the course of those years. Forty couples! That's eighty souls to minister to, forty relationships to sort out, and perhaps a number of marriages to set upon a proper foundation. Almost all pastors will perform a wedding or two each year and some will perform several each year. Pastors, then, need to anticipate the problem of cohabitation and be prepared to minister effectively.

Pastors report that cohabiting couples can come from the ranks of the church, the surrounding community, and from the "fringes" of the church—perhaps a person related to someone in the church. It's true, though, that cohabiting couples who approach the church for a wedding are *less* likely to be members or regular attendees. This is somewhat encouraging in that at least most cohabiting couples are not emerging from the "core" of the church. Still, that some cohabiting couples are members or regular attendees shows the powerful cultural influences at work today. Some churched couples can, in fact, show a remarkably casual attitude about adopting this lifestyle, confirming that a great deal of moral education concerning marriage needs to continue in the pulpits of our land.

Pastors have a responsibility to provide a thorough biblical education for their flocks, including what the Bible has to say about marriage and sexual morality. Pastors must take the lead in outlining the proper understanding of marriage, conveying such to the leadership of the church and to the congregation. At one time, the Puritans were able to provide leadership in sexual morality for the whole nation; modern pastors have trouble with their own flocks! Are we failing to indoctrinate our flocks in the biblical theology of marriage?

Certainly the prevalence of and the casual attitude toward cohabitation argues for a clear and consistent approach to these couples by pastors. Most pastors seem not to have a written policy on weddings, and those who do are impressed with how effectively they work. Thus, it seems better to be well prepared rather than be caught off guard. In appendix C of this book is included a sample wedding policy document that addresses, among other issues, cohabitation.

Pastoral Guidelines in Ministering to Cohabiting Couples

What factors need to be considered in such a policy? Building on the two broad points of the last chapter—namely, that pastors should be open to ministering to cohabiting couples and that a clear, thought-through policy ought to be in place—it is suggested that the following principles be part of any policy that deals with cohabiting couples.

Pastors Must Approach Their Responsibilities with an Intact Theology of Marriage

We must understand and embrace the nature of marriage as a covenant in the Bible. The act of marriage creates a horizontal bond of kin and family that can be ended only by death. The vows that seal this bond must be viewed as sacred and unbreakable, because God Himself seals the bond. The obligations of marriage ensue from the agreement. Covenant is also the vehicle by which God conveys His own love for us, a further reason that it must be seen as sacred. Marriage is *this* kind of covenant, with *these* elements. Further, the parties vow before God to exclusively love each other for life, and the God-given gift of the sexual relationship is not to be severed from this covenantal promise. When it is, we should view it as profaning something that God has called holy. Do we understand this and believe it?

A proper theology of marriage also understands God's purposes for marriage. As the Puritans taught, the mutual help, love, and companionship of the partners is the chief good of marriage. "It is not good that man should be alone," says the Lord. Procreation and the loving nurture of children are also in view, the goal being to produce a godly heritage. Marriage, too, is the only proper channel for the human sex drive, and volumes of material are available today on the disastrous consequences of misusing this gift. Marriage is as well the cure of sinful independence, as any married person can attest to. It is God's will that we learn to be part of a community—marriage and family being the first and foremost unit of community, then comes church, neighborhood, city, country, and world. Finally, marriage reminds us of our relationship to God. It's a reflection of the Old Testament covenant, of God's special love for His people, His unrelenting faithfulness and forgiveness, and of the permanence of the bond His people share with Him. The New Testament picture of Christ and the church also shows us the position we have in the Lord Jesus Christ. He loves us and cherishes us, which is also to be a picture of marriage.

Before we can do any effective pastoral work, we must come to it with these convictions. Many ministry situations allow pastors the opportunity to comment on God's plan for marriage. Pastors should always labor to make sure these fundamental elements are grasped by others.

The Wedding Process Should Remain Focused on a Proper Theology of Marriage

Pastors have a unique and special privilege to be welcomed to some of the most intimate and special moments in the lives of people. The wedding process is one of those. The process begins with a request for a wedding, and from that first moment, pastors must be determined to convey and teach a proper theology of marriage. Without it, the couple is not prepared and the pastor has yet to do his duty as a shepherd. Some years ago a younger widow in our church was seeing a man. She grew to care for him but was surprised when he suggested they move in together to "see if things will work out." I asked her, "What did you say to him?" She said, "I emphatically told him no. I learned many years ago that marriage is something special and doing something like that would not be right." She'd been well taught concerning the theology of marriage.

So to teach the proper view of marriage, the pastor can use all the opportunities of the premarital period: the initial interview, during premarital counseling, at the wedding rehearsal, and at the wedding itself. I do so in the very first encounters I have with couples seeking a wedding. With Bible in hand, we study together what God has said about the covenant of marriage and sexual purity. If a couple fails to grasp this concept or I'm not satisfied with their response, we do it again until they do grasp it. In the midst of this, one hopes for that holy awe that often falls on a couple when they realize, "Okay, this is it. I'm in it for life, with God as my witness. I have to do this God's way." I have now begun to cover this material thoroughly in a mandatory workshop for couples who seek a wedding in our church. I feel it is the most important dimension of my premarital pastoral counseling, because when couples internalize this truth it, more than anything else, prepares and protects them for a lifelong love relationship.

I also reiterate the theology of marriage at the wedding rehearsal in a little introduction I give before we start the rehearsal. I do so for the benefit of not only the couple but also for all the parents, attendants, and others who may be present. And, of course, in one way or another I reiterate the theology of marriage in the wedding ceremony. (Appendix D is a sample wedding ceremony, structured around the biblical notion of covenant.) With this kind of saturation, the wedding couple cannot help but understand that which is most important to understand about their wedding day. I see too much emphasis being placed today on the trivialities of the wedding event, like who sits by whom at the reception or what color the bridesmaids' dresses are. It is the work of a pastor to get the focus on what really matters: the nature of the pledge the couple makes to each other and to God. The whole process should be permeated by education in the biblical doctrine of the marriage covenant.

An Emphasis on the Covenant of Marriage Should Not Lead to a Neglect of the Nurture of Ongoing Marriage Relationships

From the marriage covenant ensues obligations that are spelled out in the Bible: love, companionship, respect, faithfulness, kindness, help, care, and so forth, over a lifetime. Thus, at the onset of the marriage, pastors should place equal emphasis on the covenant of marriage and on the nurture of the covenant throughout the marriage. As many have pointed out, the church should do whatever it can do to nurture marriages, and many books, materials, organizations, and programs can aid pastoral work in this regard.

Pastoral Authority Over Marriage Is Governed by the Larger Concerns of the Pastoral Calling

Pastors are not in the wedding business, they are in the shepherding business—the shepherding of souls. Pastors need to remember this shepherding function when they develop their policies on ministering to premarital couples and on whether or not they will sanction a marriage and perform a ceremony.

Certainly we would agree with the Reformers that it's proper for the state to have jurisdiction over marriage. Church history displays the quagmire that emerges if the church assumes jurisdiction over every marriage. Marriage is, after all, natural to all of humanity, and all marriages are ultimately a covenant with God, whether or not the couple acknowledges God. In our times, the state has assigned the role of solemnizing marriages to pastors, and such is an expectation of modern pastoral work. We must recognize, however, that pastoral jurisdiction over weddings is not as broad as that of the state. The state must marry anyone who doesn't have a legal impediment; the church and its pastors have a much higher and more specific calling.

Pastors are charged by the Scriptures to do pastoral work, which is to teach and shepherd souls. As long as a given couple is willing to put themselves under the teaching and guidance of a pastor, the pastoral calling can be fulfilled. Thus, whether we marry cohabitants depends upon the couple's willingness to put themselves under the teaching and authority of the pastor. If a couple willingly submits to spiritual and moral guidance, then perhaps, yes, the wedding process can move forward, assuming no other moral or spiritual problems are present.

Pastors should never feel unjustified, however, in refusing a wedding for a couple who are simply not disposed or not ready to cooperate with pastoral guidance. We may feel sadness over the lostness of some souls, but it is not the main business of pastoral work to merely solemnize marriages and sign marriage documents. That's the state's business.

Consider this analogy. Suppose a certain young man makes application to a Christian university. His pastor receives a recommendation form from the university in which are spelled out clear standards by which its students must abide. This pastor knows that the young man in question has little or no commitment to these standards, and his motivation in applying to the Christian university apparently is not all it should be. Should the pastor simply pass over this "problem" because it's his "job" to make such routine recommendations? Or should he attempt to seek amendment and clarification in the life of the young man in question?

Suppose he sits down with this young man to talk about the standards of the university and the young man indicates that he has no intention of keeping the standards. Should the pastor refuse to make a positive recommendation of this student since he's not at all inclined to live up to the standards? The proper course seems obvious. A pastor's calling goes beyond routine recommendations. We are called to give spiritual direction to others and to do so with *integrity*.

Should, then, a pastor's commitment to the standards of biblical marriage be any less? A couple that cannot or will not correct a less-than-scriptural view of marriage is not suitable for a Christian marriage (although they have a legal and natural right to marry), just as an otherwise qualified student may not be suitable for a Christian university (although he's free to attend another university). Do most Christian universities admit students because they merely hope the students will uphold their standards? Or do they admit them based upon some *evidence* in their lives that they will uphold those standards?

Let us not lose sight of a pastor's true work. If pastors perform a wedding without curing sick or wounded souls, have they really done sound pastoral work? To perform a wedding without moving a couple or an individual to the proper understanding of marriage, the wounded ones have, in fact, been left by the wayside. Are pastors true to their calling when they preside at an event at which attitudes and actions contradict important spiritual principles? Is that really the pastoral calling? When pastors, by looking the other way, embrace the further disintegration of marriage doctrine and commitment, are they really doing God's work?

Far better to realize that if God's grace is not yet alerting a couple to their need of moral correction or salvation, then it's best not covered by a facade of a smiling face. Because, given the present cultural context and the eternal realities, there's little to smile about. Surely unrepentant cohabitants do not seem proper candidates for a Christian wedding.

Pastors Should Not Lose Sight of the Importance of the Community of Faith in the Nurture of Marriages and Families

The Puritans had a strong emphasis on the need of the community of faith—the church, the body of Christ—to surround the family. The support and nurture of others was viewed as essential to the success of marriages. I make this case of community support with young couples. I have no interest in marrying them and then having them disappear from the church. That is one huge step down the road to disaster, since such a couple has withdrawn from Christian instruction, guidance, counsel, support, and admonition. Couples who come to me who are not yet ready to be enveloped in the body of Christ must demonstrate a willingness to be so before we can talk about a wedding. As a pastor I'm committed to building lives, marriages, and Christian homes. I am not committed to merely performing wedding ceremonies.

Some years ago, J. Grant Swank, a pastor, offered some strong thoughts on this point. Early in his ministry, Swank performed weddings for any couple who asked him. He subsequently reversed his thinking and insisted that the couples he married be Christians who are active in the body of Christ. He explains his reversal in thinking this way:

> Was I called of God to perform marriages for people in the house of the Lord when those persons had not committed their lives to the Lord? Was I to say prayers for two people who did not pray? Was I to read passages from the Bible to bride and groom knowing full well that they did not intend to build their home upon that Bible? Was I to ask these two people to utter their promises in the presence of Jesus when they did not regard Jesus as the Lord of their lives?[1]

Swank came to perceive the practice of marrying those not committed to the body of Christ as the equivalent of accepting the unregenerate into membership or baptizing one who was not a Christian. So his policy changed. He was still open to meeting with any couple for an initial interview, but instead of agreeing to marry any and all, he would invite the unconverted to attend church for at least six months before they had further discussions about a wedding.

Our culture brutalizes marriages. Sound pastoral premarital work surely includes insisting upon the need for the participatory nurture of the body of Christ. Pastors must recognize that their well-intentioned premarital work will likely not take hold without the ongoing nurture of that body. If a couple fails to see this or agree to it, the entire process of pastoral direction has then been aborted.

A Spirit of Loving Correction Must Govern the Pastor's Work with Cohabiting Couples

The lifestyle of cohabitation is, in no uncertain terms, against God, against the church, against marriage, against the family, and against all that pastoral work seeks to accomplish: to align men and women with God. Cohabitation must be corrected at the door of the church, then, if it's going to be corrected at all in our society. Cohabitation is not only sinful but likely to be disastrous for the couple, as all modern research indicates. When a pastor offers no correction to a cohabiting couple, that pastor has likely contributed to their future troubles.

Again, it is suggested that pastors, as should any Christian who advises cohabiters, firmly and clearly counsel what God's Word says about marriage and cohabitation. Pastors themselves stress how much more effective they are when, without apology or delay, they present God's truth to cohabiting couples. There can come, after all, no benefit from withholding such truth. Couples should be urged to reestablish a standard of sexual purity in their relationship, which would normally involve rectifying their sinful living arrangements. The point should be raised that one cannot expect God's blessing when there is clear disobedience to His commands. Information should be given to the couple on the problems and deficiencies of the cohabiting lifestyle so they can see that the pastor has their best interests in view. Pastors should do all this, of course, in a spirit of love and gentleness, realizing that a loving and gentle manner makes the medicine easier to take.

Cohabitants have come to the pastor, seeking something from him; it's only fair for a pastor to ask something of them—to do things God's way. I couch this discussion in terms of the couple's making their own decision, setting out God's will and plan and leaving it to the couple to decide if they want to do it His way or not. I even have a written agreement they can take and sign or not sign. Thus, the couple, not me, makes the decision on whether a wedding will happen. If they follow my direction and counsel, they display a change of heart and a willingness to be open to the proper understanding of marriage. A sample of the written agreement is in appendix C.

In this kind of patient pastoral work, pastors do the spiritual surgery that is their daily labor. Again, if cohabitation is not corrected at the front door of the church, where will it be corrected? As pastors, we ultimately seek that a couple will come out of a cohabiting lifestyle, begin to grasp God's will for marriage and sex, display remorse for their actions, and be willing to make the proper corrections in their lifestyle. Pastoral work is to shepherd souls on to God, and cohabitants present a unique challenge in this endeavor since they come to pastors often with only one thought in mind—they want a wedding. All the tact, skill, and care a Spirit-filled pastor can muster will be required for the desired outcome. In our church, we also now use a preliminary document that stresses that couples will be asked questions about their spiritual condition before we discuss weddings and dates.

For those rightly prepared to make a covenant of marriage, the pastor can lead them to it and help them go on to nurture it. For those, like many cohabitants, who are ill prepared to do so, pastors can stand ready to teach and shepherd. And some cohabiting couples who come to a pastor may be ripe for evangelism. Thus, for those who have sinned, yet have no cognizance of it, perhaps God will allow us to lead some to Him, for their own sakes and for the sakes of their marriages. Sometimes the Spirit of God uses these moments when sinfulness is confronted to begin a work of grace. In any case, in spiritual warfare there should be no surrender by God's pastoral soldiers.

Pastoral Realism in Ministering to Cohabiting Couples

We have to know what we're up against. The earlier chapters of this book made clear how widespread the practice of cohabitation is and how utterly oblivious many couples are to the moral problem it presents to Christians. It won't be easy for pastors in such an environment to do the work God has called them to do. It's likely that we'll fail more often than we'll succeed. But surely we have to try, and perhaps God will give us some victories.

One pastor told of a woman who'd grown up in his church and returned from several years in college with a young man, seeking to be married. Upon learning that they were living together, the pastor specified his conditions, including separate residences and a reestablishment of sexual purity. They left chagrined but promising to consider it. The pastor never heard from them again. Her family left the church, and another local pastor agreed to do the wedding, labeling the initial pastor as narrow-minded. Such scenarios are unfortunate but probably not uncommon. The first pastor later remarked, however, that he was thankful that his conscience was clear in the matter. And in pastoral work, a clear conscience is worth more than just about anything. We will, after all, stand before Christ one day to give account of our work.

Another pastor married a couple who'd been cohabiting, not demanding any corrective action. The marriage quickly ended in divorce and the parties returned to their former lifestyle, only this time with other partners. The pastor regretted performing the wedding and determined from then on to adopt a policy requiring cohabiting couples to separate to "prove their commitment to what is right in God's eyes." Many pastors have learned that, without corrective action, individuals will not likely undergo a true change during the premarital process, thereby, as statistics indicate, endangering their marriages.

Another pastor, as a favor, married a cohabiting couple who lived next door to him. They were friends of the pastor but not believers. This couple has now been married for some years but they still have not come to faith; they haven't even been in the church since the wedding. Pastors sometimes think that by doing such favors, the couple will become Christians. But it may not work out that way. Pastors, rather, should look for clear evidence of the work of the Spirit of God. Merely trying to be someone's friend doesn't accomplish pastoral work.

Yet another pastor was visited by a young couple who came to him seeking a wedding, bringing with them their eighteen-month-old son. The pastor explained his policies: an entire premarital program and a requirement to live separately and in purity until the wedding. They declined and were married elsewhere, but he offered premarital counseling anyway. They again refused, and later went through a "rancorous" divorce. Many cohabiting couples are not prepared for marriage, even if a child is present, and difficult as it may be in some situations, it's imperative that they receive counsel and correction.

Clearly, many pastors have had difficult experiences in seeking to minister to cohabiting couples. One pastor said, "All of my experiences have been less than rewarding." Another said, "I wish I had an example of a situation of successful ministry to a cohabiting couple. I do not." One pastor concluded some written remarks to me with these mournful comments: "This area is the most personally discouraging of any area of the ministry. Mothers will lie to you, brides will be pregnant without telling you, divorces will happen within six months of the wedding . . . and above all, the church where you are serving doesn't give a hoot."

It's not impossible, though, to observe rewards in this kind of pastoral work. Thus, pastors would be wise not to get discouraged over situations that are less than successful. We are ministering today in a culture that provides sizable challenges for a pastor seeking to teach God's will concerning marriage. We'll encounter faulty morality, secularized thinking, and a desire to be served. Pastors, though, must concentrate on ministering faithfully, and accept the defeats as well as the victories. In a fallen world, even the soundest pastoral work will, many times, fall short of the desired result.

On the other hand, some days will bring glorious victory. A pastor was able to lead a man to Christ who, with his cohabiting partner, had come to him about a wedding. They agreed to move apart and enthusiastically engaged in a lengthy premarital counseling program. The woman, who was a backslidden Christian, came back to the Lord and has become a spokesperson for sexual purity in their community. Theirs was a case of clear and abiding repentance, which is what pastors must always pray for, work for, and hope for.

Another couple began attending a church while they were living together. They both came to Christ and were brought into a discipleship Bible study. By the time they came to the pastor, they'd been convicted of their sin and, of their own accord, had lived apart and restored sexual purity in their relationship. They're faithfully serving the Lord many years later. These examples show the power of the Word of God in lives that are truly born again of the Spirit. Pastors must not cease to labor for a demonstration of the power of God to change lives by His Spirit.

One pastor didn't discover that a couple in his church was living together until a new church directory came out; the man and woman had the same address. The pastor made up his mind to contact this couple, and in the meantime they came to him to talk about a wedding. They confessed that they were living together and, although initially resistant, they complied with a requirement to live apart until the ceremony. They established and maintained a standard of purity and later, when they told their story to the church, it had a profound impact.

There are many "success stories" of couples and individuals coming to Christ as they approach pastors for weddings. There are also many "success stories" of repentance and changed lives. So pastors might be heartened by noting that success does occur. Even in the modern world, repentance and changed lives must be the sum and substance of pastoral work. These success stories should encourage pastors to firmly minister the Word of God. Rather than settle for wedding ceremonies, pastors should continue to seek to amend lives.

Many other comments made by pastors are worth noting. Several said that determining the proper course of action in some situations can be excruciating. Ministering in today's world, with all its moral and personal contortions, will present vexing dilemmas. Thus, we as pastors should not judge one another harshly in these matters. Other pastors remarked that when a couple does choose to right themselves after cohabiting, tremendous changes often take place in their lives. The couples tend to experience a great sense of victory, and these changes build a wonderful foundation for marriage. On the other hand, some couples will choose to go elsewhere when they meet with counsel that comes from the Scriptures. Pastors have no control over what is in a couple's hearts and have to accept such decisions.

Pastor Jim Cymbala of the Brooklyn Tabernacle relates a significant cohabiting story in his book *Fresh Wind, Fresh Fire* about the history of his church.[2] A couple came forward during an altar call. They were fashionable in appearance, and the woman asked for prayer. When Pastor Cymbala asked what to pray for, she answered that she wanted prayer for their relationship. Pastor Cymbala sought further information and learned they were living together. He replied with these words:

> Okay, that puts me in sort of a bind. You want me to ask God to bless something that He has already expressed His opinion about. He's already made it clear in the Bible that living together outside of marriage is wrong. So it looks like to me I'd be wasting everybody's time to ask His help in this situation, wouldn't I? I'll tell you what— let's get on track with God's plan. . . . How about you finding another place to live right now? You say you want God's best for your relationship. Okay, this is step number one. This will open the door for many other good things.[3]

Initially the couple wasn't thrilled with this blunt approach, but finally they agreed. Pastor Cymbala had it right, and his counsel was correct. There was little else he could have or should have said. And he readily admitted that he hasn't always had success in this approach, but in being true to his own conscience and calling, he succeeded this day as he spoke the truth in love. The couple in question went on to receive counseling through the church and, in the conclusion to a dramatic story, were wed before fifteen hundred people at the tabernacle's weekly prayer meeting.

Aiming for God's high standards will not always meet with success, but will allow for some great days of victory when those standards become the fountainhead of repentance and earnest desire. Such is the business of every pastor and every Christian. When we encounter cohabiting couples, we should love them enough to aim for no lower than God's best—repentance and a turning to seek God's good and perfect plan for their lives.

Chapter 12

Pastoral Counseling with Couples Who Have Cohabited

A recent article in the *Wall Street Journal* outlined the growing push for expanded legal rights on behalf of cohabiting couples.[1] More municipalities, for example, have created a "registry" where "domestic partners" can make their status "official." In some places this might make them eligible for benefits or protections reserved for spouses. The American Law Institute—an influential organization of lawyers, judges, and legal scholars—is also recommending broad changes in family law to accommodate unmarried people living together. And many corporations have acted to expand benefits for unmarried partners. And, "Why not?" the thinking goes. According to the 2000 U.S. census, more than five million couples are cohabiting. Should they not get the same legal protections and other benefits afforded to married couples—health insurance benefits, health club memberships, power of attorney? There's a strong push in this direction.

As I looked closer at the article, however, I realized that this "push" hasn't yet made the substantial progress that the tone of the article suggests. Many of the accommodations thus far have been largely symbolic, something the author of the article admits. And the article concludes by strongly suggesting that couples who are living together without the benefit of marriage form "cohabitation agreements"— legal documents that outline the rights and protections of each party to the agreement regarding finances, assets, parental rights, bill-paying, and so forth, and covers both the duration of cohabitation and after. Perhaps all these rights for cohabiting couples are not quite so imminent if there's still a need for these agreements. In truth, there's still substantial reluctance in our society to equate cohabitation to marriage.

The reader by now grasps the hazards of the cohabiting lifestyle. And what folly it is that leads many in our society to push for changes that make this choice even more accommodating and more inviting! I personally hope these efforts fail and that municipalities, corporations, legislatures, and other institutions realize that the cohabiting lifestyle is harming people rather than helping them. And these "people" include many children who become the victims of volatile and unstable relationships. We need, rather, to promote marriage, properly understood as being in the long-term best interests of individuals, couples, and children, as well as society as a whole. Nevertheless, cohabitation continues to be an increasingly popular choice across our land. Thus, in the years to come pastors will encounter more and more couples whose marriages are in trouble owing, at least in part, to their marriages being built upon the foundation of cohabitation.

Greg and Jean came to me some years ago. They'd been married for about ten years and seemed the typical suburban-type couple— educated and affluent. Greg owned a successful business and Jean was a professor. They were now in their midthirties, and it became evident as I talked with them that they were having severe marital problems. Their marriage had, in fact, been highly volatile since the beginning, with frequent outbursts, heated arguments, and even some physical violence. They had two children and desperately wanted to get along and stay together. They also seemed to have a measure of affection and love for each other. Both of them were Christians, active in their church and its ministries, and they were deeply embarrassed by what was going on between them.

To make a long story short, the root of their long-term marital discord was planted early in their relationship when they had cohabited prior to marriage, and the problems they experienced in their marriage clearly stemmed from their period of cohabitation. During counseling, I outlined what I perceived as the major issues:

1. *Independence and power.* Both Greg and Jean were very independent and neither liked giving in to the other. They maintained a certain independent spirit that carried over from their cohabiting days.
2. *Weak commitment.* The first time I met with them, they both viewed divorce as the most likely scenario. They didn't have a deep sense that they'd be successful in working through their problems, and they had little hope or determination.
3. *Poor understanding of marriage.* They indicated that they'd had no sound premarital counseling that clearly outlined what marriage was all about.
4. *Impurity.* Both Greg and Jean expressed that in the past they'd come pretty close to adulterous relationships with coworkers and others they spent a lot of time with. Each found this deeply hurtful.

Perhaps 50 percent of couples who cohabit go on to marry, although this number seems to be declining. And Greg and Jean had fallen into an all-too-typical syndrome of couples in that category. The independent spirit that Greg and Jean carried into their marriage manifested itself in many ways: a lack of support for one another in career decisions, a refusal to help each other with their individual problems, a constant release of angry and hurtful words and actions, and so forth. Their lack of commitment to their marriage, despite their

Christian faith and the presence of two small children, led them to being strongly attracted to others of the opposite sex. Nor were they committed to purity of life. All of these problems emerged quite naturally and logically from their earlier cohabiting experience. Cohabitation fosters, after all, individualism rather than mutuality, involves only the most modest kind of commitment—that we will live together for a time but with the understanding that either party can walk away—and involves sexually immoral behavior. Apart from deep repentance, a person who embraces sexual immorality will often return to it. Do we think, then, that all of these underlying realities will just disappear once a wedding ceremony takes place?

So how do we minister to a couple like Greg and Jean? Certainly we need to recognize that the situations of cohabiting couples differ, and good pastoral counselors must probe deeply into the lives they have before them in order to discern the particular realities a given couple presents. But some general guidelines can help us with couples who once cohabited and who now—confused, troubled, and broken over a marriage that's gone bad—show up in the pastor's study. Behind all the sorrowful statistics, behind the volatility and disintegration of relationships begun in cohabitation, are lives—lives that are in trouble and misery. And a pastor's work will intersect such lives today. How can we help couples like Greg and Jean restore their marriage relationships? Following are five guidelines.

Thoroughly Probe the Beginnings of the Relationship, Including the Attitudes That Led the Couple to Cohabit and Later to Marry

Why did a couple cohabit in the first place? And why did they finally marry? The reasons a couple sought marriage often may not rise to the level of God's wisdom. They may have conceived a child. They may have reached a certain age. Family pressures may have mounted. Or they genuinely believed at the time that they were in love and that their relationship should progress to marriage. But even this is not a sufficient mind-set. They may not have begun their marriage with the helpful conviction that God wanted them together. Probing the reasons for cohabitation and later marriage should give pastors insight to help the couple see how their relationship was built on a faulty foundation from the beginning. The revelation can be painful but is absolutely necessary.

Determine the Commitment Level of Their Marriage

How committed to their marriage was the couple at the time of their wedding, all through the years, and now at the most recent moment? I have couples rate commitment on a scale of one to ten—not committed at all (1) to absolutely committed (10). This information is important, suggesting to the pastoral counselor if a weak commitment to marriage is at the root of some of a couple's problems. Such is often so for couples who have cohabited in the past. Sometimes these couples reach a better understanding of marriage and they seem quite committed to a lifelong partnership. If so, then, perhaps the counseling should move in another direction. Many of these couples, though, feel quite hopeless about the marriage because their commitment and confidence is weak.

Lay Out What You Believe the Deficiencies to Be, and Reteach a Biblical Theology of Marriage

Share with the couple where you see cracks in the foundation of the marriage, then begin training them in the biblical teaching of marriage. Point out to struggling couples that when people enter matrimony with an intact theology of marriage it's of great help in working through the hard times and constructively resolving issues. A couple may not realize what they've done to their relationship in the decision to cohabit. Specifically, show couples the clear difference between the immoral and casual nature of cohabitation and the lofty holiness of marriage. Help them understand the nature of a one-flesh relationship and how it creates a kinship bond that cannot be broken. Explain the principle of a covenant; that regardless of their understanding at the time, they did indeed make promises to God that He Himself witnessed and sealed. They may need to correct their attitude regarding their original reason for marrying, which leads to the next point. In time, they might feel led to renew their vows with a deepened and corrected understanding.

Help Them Make a Thorough Confession to One Another and to God

Ask couples to develop a list of specific ways they've sinned against God's ordinance of marriage and the ways this hurts their spouses. Some people may have to confess that they "used" their spouses prior to marriage and that this attitude carried into the marriage. Also, they certainly have to confess sexual sin, and some may have been promiscuous or serial cohabiters prior to their current relationships. These past sins may need to be exposed and repented of if the present relationship is going to heal. They may have to agree with God that they did not respect His ordinance of marriage and, even though they went on to marry, they didn't give proper weight to the meaning of the bond of marriage. They may have to admit the sinfulness of their independent spirit and how wrong and destructive it's been in their marriage. Encourage the confession to continue until consciences are clear and forgiveness has been extended. Couples probably should have some genuine sorrow over their failure to being a proper partner in the marriage. The apostle Paul reminds us of the power of the cleansed life: "For godly sorrow produces repentance leading to salvation, not to be regretted. . . . For observe this very thing, that you sorrowed in a godly manner: What diligence it produced in you, what clearing of yourselves, what indignation, what fear, what vehement desire, what zeal, what vindication!" (2 Cor. 7:10–11). Yes, couples who have cohabited need practical guidance and suggestions on how to have a better relationship. But those who have been ensnared in the sin of cohabitation need a deep cleansing in the grace of God and a heartfelt willingness to extend forgiveness to the partner. A thorough repentance is often key in restoring such relationships. If a troubled couple can begin to reach this level and communicate with one another in these terms, the healing has begun.

Lead the Couple to Recommit Themselves to a Lifelong Covenant of Marriage

This recommitment can be done quietly in prayer with the pastor leading the couple to God's throne right in a living room or a pastor's study. Or it can be done in a more formal setting that includes the restating of wedding vows (this time with the proper understanding). I have presided at the latter on a few occasions, and it can be a most blessed experience for the couple willing to do it. A recommitment to the covenant, coupled with some kind of public confession or testimony, can be glorious and powerful, too, in the life of the church. Seek, of course, what couples are prepared to do and be sensitive to their wishes. The important thing is that restoration occurs in their lives and in their marriages.

These steps form a broad outline for sound pastoral work with couples who have cohabited in the past. Certainly there will be many variables. But this process offers troubled couples hope that they can reach the place they long to be in their relationship. I helped Greg and Jean work through some of these principles. They did stay together and they did rebuild their marriage. They recommitted themselves to each other, this time with the proper understanding. They saw the volatility of their relationship decrease as they learned to help and support one another in the spirit of Genesis chapter 2. They discovered experientially what a good plan God has for marriages, and they found new depths to their love of each other, which dimmed any longings and temptations they had for others. In the end, they gained God's best.

Cohabitation does not necessarily doom anyone to misery, trouble, violence, and divorce for the rest of their lives. The grace of God is greater than all our sin. There is hope. Even those who have sinned in this way can be restored to the full blessing of what God desires for us in marriage. Some couples are able to get to this place themselves, but many need help. This help is often the work of a pastor.

The 2003 film featuring the life of Thomas "Stonewall" Jackson— *Gods and Generals*—tells the story of this very interesting figure in civil war history. Eccentric and driven, Jackson was a devout, Bible-quoting man, despite his legendary and sometimes ruthless work as a general in the Civil War. The film displays the depth of Jackson's love affair with his wife Anna. Presumably historically accurate, the film shows a man and woman deeply in love, communicating on a deep and tender level, and relishing that they will be together in this life and the next. Although Jackson did not live long, he did experience what God intended in his marriage: a love relationship with his spouse that extended through their too-brief years together on earth. I suggest that their profound love developed primarily because Jackson and Anna did things God's way, following the teachings of God's Word.

Doing things God's way is what this book ultimately has been about. Cohabitation is *not* God's way. Covenant marriage *is* God's way. And it's the work of pastors, by God's grace, to effect change and amendment in the lives of those ensnared in the harmful and sinful web of cohabitation. Let us always be mindful, "The fear of the LORD is the beginning of wisdom" (Prov. 1:7).

Cohabitation Facts

1. Percentage of couples who are cohabiting at any one time: 5 percent.
2. Percentage of Americans who have cohabited at some time: 50 percent.
3. Percentage of cohabiting couples who go on to marry: 50–60 percent.
4. Percentage of cohabiting couples who have been married previously: at least 30 percent.
5. Percentage of never-married individuals between twenty-five and thirty-four in a cohabiting relationship: 20–24 percent.
6. Percentage of cohabiting relationships involving children: 40 percent.
7. Percentage of children born to cohabiting couples who will experience the termination of their parents' relationship (splitting up or divorce): 75 percent.
8. Average length of a cohabiting relationship that does not lead to marriage: 12–18 months.

9. Percentage of unions that survive two years:
   - cohabiting unions not leading to marriage: 33 percent.
   - marital unions: 95 percent.
10. Percentage of unions that survive ten years:
    - cohabiting unions not leading to marriage: 12 percent.
    - marital unions: 90 percent.
11. Likelihood of divorce: Within the first ten years of marriage, those who cohabit prior to marriage are almost twice as likely to divorce as opposed to those who do not cohabit prior to marriage.
12. Likelihood of marital disruption within the first ten years:
    - cohabited prior to marriage: 57 percent.
    - did not cohabit prior to marriage: 30 percent.
13. Likelihood of marital disruption within the first two years of marriage:
    - cohabited prior to marriage: 29 percent.
    - did not cohabit prior to marriage: 9 percent.
14. Percentage of Americans who believe cohabitation is morally wrong: 25 percent.
15. Additional percentage of Americans who have some moral qualms about cohabitation: 25 percent.
16. Percentage of Americans over age 60 who approve of cohabitation: 20 percent.
17. Married couples who believe that the likelihood of experiencing a divorce in their relationship is "very low:"
    - those who cohabited prior to marriage: 39 percent.
    - those who did not cohabit prior to marriage: 61 percent.

Pastoral Remarks to Cohabiting Couples

You are living together. As you might imagine, that's a bit of a problem from a pastor's point of view. Three reasons come to mind that strongly suggest you reconsider your decision to live together. First, according to the Bible, living together before marriage is clearly characterized as a form of immorality or sexual sin. The Bible says it should not even be named as among Christians. I realize it's a very popular practice today, but it's not at all pleasing to God or in line with His desires. And our church tries to live by God's Word and God's commands.

Second, living together before marriage goes directly against God. He ordained marriage as the foundation of all society and called it sacred. It is to be reverenced and respected, and your actions have disrespected it. You have come here to have a church wedding, desiring God's blessing, but you're not doing things the way God said to do them. Does that make any sense? Let's read Hebrews 13:4: "Marriage is honorable among all, and the bed undefiled; but fornicators and adulterers God will judge." When you cohabit, you put yourself in direct opposition to God, who longs for marriage to be honored. I realize you may intend to be married at some point, but so long as you cohabit you show disrespect for God's command. It's not only a bad example for others but a form of direct rebellion against God.

A third reason it would be wise to reconsider cohabiting is what you've done to your own hopes for a good marriage. Cohabitation has proven to be very risky in terms of future marital happiness. For example, couples who cohabit prior to marriage are more likely to be unhappy in marriage and more likely to be unfaithful to their partners. Couples who cohabit prior to marriage, when tracked over ten years, are about twice as likely to divorce than those who do not cohabit. Within the first two years of marriage, almost a third of such couples will be divorced. Sociological studies have proven that cohabitation is a bad idea in terms of future marital success. Particular elements of cohabitation corrupt the ability to have a long-term happy and successful relationship. In our counseling together, we can talk about those elements and perhaps gain insight into them.

I say all this in your best interest. I'm not picking on you. Any cohabiting couple is in the same boat. The simple fact is that cohabiting tends to lay an unsound foundation for marriage. So the harmful elements of cohabitation need careful correction, and you now have an opportunity to correct them. So the pastors at First Church advise cohabiting couples to do two things. First, we ask you to make a strong commitment to the premarital counseling process. Both the counseling and the commitment to it are critically important for you. Second, we ask you to seek a repentant spirit. We want you to make a decision to do things God's way for the remaining time of your premarital state. That means making arrangements to live apart and reestablishing a standard of sexual purity in your relationship.

I know that sounds like a lot, but it will give back to your relationship so much. You will once again build your relationship on companionship rather than easy sex. You will create in your hearts a longing for marriage—your marriage later on will feel like liberation rather than a trap. You will also have the opportunity to view your relationship with a new objectivity and begin to correct some of the damaging attitudes and issues that cohabitation tends to cause. You will build trust. Your consciences will be clear. You will begin to build your relationship on a foundation that will last a lifetime. By living apart and reestablishing a new pattern of sexual purity, you'll be amazed at the positive changes it brings about in your relationship. We've never heard of a couple taking this step and regretting it. Yes, it's a hard step, but many, many couples have enjoyed putting this special part of their relationship back under God's control. This is our expectation and our hope for you.

A Sample Church Wedding Policy

Weddings at First Church

At First Church, marriage is viewed as a sacred covenant. In the Bible, marriage is called a covenant, which is a special kind of promise, one in which God Himself is the witness. The bride and groom take vows, which God seals. The result is that husband and wife are joined for life, beginning a lifelong bond of family and kinship that can be broken only by death. It's imperative that couples do more than merely plan a wedding ceremony; they must prepare for a love relationship over a lifetime. In fulfilling the responsibilities of Christian marriage and building a Christian home, a couple ensures many benefits that will impact their own lives, the lives of their children, and the lives of others. As we begin the process of establishing a Christian marriage, we make the first steps toward building a godly heritage.

The Wedding Process at First Church

1. When requesting a wedding, couples meet with a pastoral staff member for an initial interview and review all First Church wedding policies.

2. Couples are asked to make steps to conform to all requirements set forth in the policies.
3. Couples sign and return premarital covenant.
4. A couple's wedding is placed on the church calendar.
5. Couples engage in premarital counseling with staff pastor.
6. Couples attend wedding rehearsal; couples are joined at wedding event.

First Church Pastoral Wedding Policies

Every couple seeking a wedding at First Church should ask themselves a question: Are you merely seeking a wedding ceremony or are you seeking to prepare for the responsibilities of Christian marriage and building a Christian home? Couples should recognize that the calling of the pastors of First Church is such that we are focused on the latter. Consequently, our policies are in line with this objective.

1. The parties must demonstrate a genuinely submissive spirit to the pastoral guidance they receive.
2. The couple must agree to several required premarital counseling sessions (as many as the pastor deems necessary).
3. The couple will be expected to understand and embrace a biblical covenant of marriage (a commitment for life, vowed before God).
4. Both parties must give evidence of saving faith in Christ. This is more than nominal Christian faith. Both parties must be born again of the Spirit, having personally trusted in Jesus Christ for salvation.
5. Given the clear statement of Scripture, our pastors cannot marry a believer to one who is not yet a believer.
6. Given the importance of the nurture of Christian marriages, couples must evidence a commitment to active participation

in the body of Christ, our own church, or another like-minded congregation.

7. As God's Word states that sexual purity before marriage is the only acceptable standard, couples are asked to establish and maintain such a standard in their relationship.

8. Couples who are living together will be expected to make arrangements to establish separate residences, and then to recommit to and maintain sexual purity for the duration of the preparation process.

9. If there is divorce in the background of either party, this should be made known immediately to the pastor. These couples will be referred to a separate handout titled "Divorce and Remarriage at First Church."

10. Couples will be asked to sign a premarital covenant agreement. Only after this step is taken will a wedding date be confirmed on the church calendar.

11. Couples are expected to maintain a cooperative spirit with the pastors and wedding coordinator in the fulfillment of all other nonpastoral policies regarding the wedding preparations and wedding events.

Premarital Covenant Agreement

- We have read and agree to fulfill all of the wedding policies set forth by First Church.
- We agree to submit to the pastoral direction given to us.
- We agree to actively participate in the believing community now and after our marriage.
- We agree to maintain a standard of sexual purity throughout the time of our courtship.
- We agree to make a vow to God for a lifetime covenant of marriage.

- We agree to enthusiastically engage in the premarital preparation and counseling process.

Signed: _____
(Groom)

Signed: _____
(Bride)

Signed: _____
(Parent of Groom)

Signed: _____
(Parent of Bride)

Upon receipt of this signed covenant, the wedding can be placed on the church calendar. Our pastors retain the right to end the premarital process and cancel First Church's participation in the wedding if this agreement is not sincerely fulfilled.

A Sample Church Wedding Ceremony

The Covenant of Marriage

Opening Remarks

Welcome friends and family. We are gathered here to join this man and this woman in the sacred bond of marriage. In the Bible, marriage is presented as a covenant. A covenant is a special kind of promise, one in which God Himself is witness. In this covenant of marriage today, _____ and _____ will make a special oath, a vow to God, that God Himself will seal. God will ever be the third strand of the marriage braid. The result will be that _____ and _____ will be joined together for life as husband and wife. Between them God creates a horizontal and permanent bond of kin and family.

Therefore, in the biblical understanding, to enter upon marriage is to renounce the possibility of ever leaving it. I am satisfied that _____ and _____ understand this and are pledging this kind of covenant today. And we trust that the bond created today by these vows will bring to their lives all that God intends: love, mutual help and companionship, the loving nurture of children, the enjoyment of one another, and a lasting, godly heritage. These things reflect God's purposes for marriage. Behind the events of marriage lay a picture of God's own relationship with His people, a covenantal relationship. May this union be a true picture of God's own covenant love for us and a picture of the Lord Jesus' love for His church. If anyone can show just cause why these may not be lawfully joined together, let him now speak or else forever hold his peace. . . . Who gives this woman to be married to this man?

Later Remarks to the Congregation

Family and friends, _____ and _____ are about to take their marriage vows. This will formalize and solemnize their covenant of marriage, with God as witness. It is, as always, an awesome moment, as God joins them together. Someday, when they are tempted not to keep their vows, it is then when their vows will keep them. No one can predict what challenges, trials, or seasons a long life will bring this couple, but we know that these vows, forming a covenant, will keep their love safe over all the years God gives them together.

In wedding events, we use many symbols. All of these symbols reflect the marriage covenant. _____ and _____ will exchange rings. Rings are symbols of something that has no end.

_____ and _____ today make a *lifelong* covenant, until death parts them. Their vow is for life.

_____ and _____ will also extinguish the two candles and light the unity candle. This symbolizes that their covenant is a covenant of *companionship*. According to the Bible the primary purpose of marriage is love, companionship, and support for one another.

_____ and _____ pledge today to be loving companions for life.

Later on, _____ and _____ will also sign their marriage license. This symbolizes that their covenant is a *binding* covenant. They have fulfilled all legal and social requirements and purposefully agree to enter into this bond. They intend to form a covenant of marriage today.

Also, as devoted Christians _____ and _____ acknowledge the place of Jesus Christ in their lives as Lord and Savior. Their covenant thus is also a *spiritual* covenant. It is living and active, just as their relationship with Jesus Christ. This dynamic, spiritual covenant will provide for the growth, love, and trust that will grow beautifully over a lifetime. It will protect their love over a lifetime.

Finally, _____ and _____ also stand here today with their families. They express their thanks to their loved ones for all that has been done for them as they embark on their new life together. Thus their covenant is a *new* covenant. Today is the first day in building and continuing a heritage that is meant to please and honor God.

So this covenant, sealed by these vows, witnessed by God Himself is most significant. It is a lifelong covenant and a covenant of companionship. It is a binding covenant, a spiritual covenant, and a new covenant. It is larger than these two people, as sacred as God Himself who ordained this ordinance, and it will keep these two safe and secure in their pledge to one another. And you are witnesses as God joins them together.

Remarks to the Couple

_____ and _____, in a moment I will ask you to make sacred vows and promises in the sight of God and these witnesses. You understand the commitment you are making today in your covenant of marriage. A covenant has been passed to you. It has been passed to you by God's Word, by the church of Jesus Christ, and by the legacy of centuries of Christians who have kept their marriage vows. And you are to complete your covenant, fulfilling it and nurturing it by loving and cherishing one another so long as your lives shall last.

- Promises
- Vows
- Rings

Endnotes

Introduction

1. Names and details of individuals cited in the text have been changed throughout the book in order to protect their privacy.
2. Although this is an exaggeration, it may be surprising to note that according to one researcher, studies can be cited to show that as many as 30–40 percent of college students are cohabiting at any given time. Roland H. Johnson III, "Cohabitation (good for him, not for her)." Personal remarks from an address posted at http://personalwebs.myriad.net/Roland/cohab1.htm, p. 1, accessed 2 July 2002.
3. L. L. Bumpass, J. A. Sweet, and A. Cherlin, "The Role of Cohabitation in the Declining Rates of Marriage," *Journal of Marriage and Family* 53 (1991): 914.
4. Karen S. Peterson, "Cohabiting Can Make Marriage an Iffy Proposition," *USA Today*, 8 July 2002, 1.
5. Michael J. McManus, *Marriage Savers* (Grand Rapids: Zondervan, 1995), 12.

Chapter 1: What Is a Cohabiting Couple?

1. The landmark case of Marvin versus Marvin in 1976, in which
    actor Lee Marvin's live-in companion was awarded compensa-
    tion, allowed unmarried cohabitants to sue for division of prop-
    erty. See C. L. Cole, "The Future of Cohabitation," *Alternative
    Lifestyles* 4 (1981): 524. This case was decided, however, on the
    basis of property law and did not involve any fundamental shift
    in marriage or family law. Many in the legal profession have called
    for a greater response to the "rights" of unmarried couples, but
    there have been few developments in this area. Subsequent court
    rulings have rather persistently held that the rights found natu-
    rally in a marital relationship are not transferable to couples who
    merely live together. See www.palimony.com/12.html for a chro-
    nological summary of such court rulings in California.

2. American Bar Association, *Your Legal Guide to Marriage and Other
    Relationships,* Public Education Division (Chicago: American
    Bar Association, 1989).

3. P. G. Jackson, "On Living Together Unmarried," *Journal of
    Family Issues* 4 (1983): 39.

4. M. A. Lamanna and A. Riedmann, *Marriages and Families: Mak-
    ing Choices and Facing Change* (Belmont, Calif.: Wadsworth,
    1994), 170.

5. Julie Scelfo, "Love—and Marriage?" *Newsweek,* 2 December
    2002, 9.

6. Roland H. Johnson III, remarks from an address titled "Co-
    habitation (good for him, not for her)" available at http://
    personalwebs.myriad.net/Roland/cohab1.htm, accessed 2 July
    2002.

7. Scott Stanley quoted in Karen S. Peterson, "Cohabiting Can Make
    Marriage an Iffy Proposition," *USA Today,* 8 July 2002, 2.

8. R. R. Rindfuss and A. VandenHeuval, "Cohabitation: A Pre-
    cursor to Marriage or an Alternative to Being Single?" in *The

Changing American Family: Sociological and Demographic Perspectives,
ed. S. J. South and S. E. Tolnay (Boulder, Colo.: Westview,
1992), 121–38.

9. Johnson, "Cohabitation (good for him, not for her)," 5.
10. Ibid., 8.

Chapter 2: How Many Cohabiting Couples Are There?

1. M. A. Lamanna and A. Riedmann, *Marriages and Families: Making Choices and Facing Change* (Belmont, Calif.: Wadsworth,
1994), 168.
2. Ibid., 214–15.
3. P. C. Glick and G. B. Spanier, "Married and Unmarried Cohabitation in the United States," *Journal of Marriage and the Family*
42 (1980): 20.
4. G. B. Spanier, "Married and Unmarried Cohabitation in the
United States," *Journal of Marriage and the Family* 45 (1983): 277.
The number of couples cohabiting at any one time is a much
different statistic from the number of people who have cohabited at some time.
5. Ibid., 279.
6. J. A. Sweet, "Differentials in the Approval of Cohabitation,"
NSFH Working Paper, no. 8 (Madison: University of Wisconsin-Madison, Center for Demography and Ecology, 1989), 1.
7. L. J. Waite, "Does Marriage Matter?" *Demography* 32 (1995): 485.
8. B. D. Whitehead and D. Popenoe, "The State of Our Unions:
Unmarried Cohabitation," *The National Marriage Project,* 2002,
1, at http://marriage.Rutgers.edu/TEXTSOOU2002.htm, accessed 2 July 2002.
9. Ibid.
10. Ibid., 2.
11. George Barna, *The Future of the American Family* (Chicago:
Moody, 1993), 120.

12. J. A. Sweet and L. L. Bumpass, "Religious Differentials in Marriage Behavior and Attitudes," *NSFH Working Paper,* no. 15 (Madison: University of Wisconsin-Madison, Center for Demography and Ecology, 1990), 156.

13. Julie Scelfo, "Love—and Marriage?" *Newsweek,* 2 December 2002, 9.

14. See Linda Waite and Maggie Gallagher, *The Case for Marriage* (New York: Doubleday, 2000).

15. S. Kurtz, "What Harvard Finds Unfit to Print," *The Wall Street Journal,* 18 October 2000.

16. Waite, "Does Marriage Matter?"

17. Ibid., 498.

18. Ibid., 499.

19. Quoted in Terry Mattingly, "Pastors Often Turn Blind Eye on Cohabiting," *The Peoria Journal Star,* 21 August 2002.

20. G. Jenkins, *Cohabitation: A Biblical Perspective* (Bramcote, Nottingham, England: Grove Books, 1992).

21. Jonathan Alter, "Get Married, Madonna," *Newsweek,* 29 April 1997, 51.

Chapter 3: Why Are Couples Cohabiting?

1. L. L. Bumpass, J. A. Sweet, and A. Cherlin, "The Role of Cohabitation in Declining Rates of Marriage," *Journal of Marriage and the Family* 53 (1991): 920.

2. C. L. Cole, "Cohabitation in Social Context," in *Marriage and Alternatives: Exploring Intimate Relationships,* ed. R. W. Libby and R. N. Whitehurst (Glenview, Ill.: Foresman and Co., 1977), 70.

3. A. L. Cotton-Huston, G. S. Lunney, and E. Heard, "This is my . . . : How Cohabitants Introduce Their Partners," *Alternative Lifestyles* 6 (1984): 209–16.

4. See, for example, Dorian Solot and Marshall Miller, *Unmarried to Each Other: The Essential Guide to Living Together as an Unmarried Couple* (New York: Marlowe and Co., 2002).

5. R. Schoen and D. Owens, "A Further Look at First Unions and First Marriages," in *The Changing American Family: Sociological and Demographic Perspectives,* ed. S. J. South and S. E. Tolnay (Boulder, Colo.: Westview, 1992), 116.
6. G. Jenkins, *Cohabitation: A Biblical Perspective* (Bramcote, Nottingham, England: Grove Books, 1992), 21.
7. George Barna, *The Future of the American Family* (Chicago: Moody, 1993), 127.
8. M. Schaffer, "Marriage Proposal," *U.S. News and World Report,* 11 March 2002, 26.
9. Ibid.
10. M. Kotkin, "To Marry or Live Together?" *Lifestyles: A Journal of Changing Patterns* 7 (1985): 167.
11. Jenkins, *Cohabitation,* 5.
12. Karen S. Peterson, "Cohabiting Can Make Marriage an Iffy Proposition," *USA Today,* 8 July 2002, 2.
13. M. D. Newcomb, "Relationship Qualities of Those Who Live Together," *Alternative Lifestyles* 6 (1983): 79.

Chapter 4: The Consequences of Cohabiting: The Conventional Wisdom

1. W. G. Axinn and A. Thornton, "The Relationship Between Cohabitation and Divorce: Selectivity or Causal Influence?" *Demography* 29 (1992): 358.
2. M. D. Newcomb and P. M. Bentler, "Cohabitation Before Marriage: A Comparison of Married Couples Who Did and Did Not Cohabit," *Alternative Lifestyles* 41 (1980): 82–83.
3. R. E. L. Watson, "Premarital Cohabitation Versus Traditional Courtship: The Effects on Subsequent Marital Adjustment," *Family Relations* 32 (1981): 139–47.
4. J. D. Teachman and K. A. Polonko, "Cohabitation and Marital Stability in the United States," *Social Forces* 69 (1990): 19.

5. A. DeMaris and G. R. Leslie, "Cohabitation with the Future Spouse: Its Influence upon Marital Satisfaction and Communication," *Journal of Marriage and the Family* 46 (1984): 83.

6. A. Greeley, *Faithful Attraction* (New York: Tom Doherty, 1991), 206.

7. Linda Waite quoted in Karen S. Peterson, "Changing the Shape of the American Family," *USA Today,* 18 April 2000, D2.

8. George Barna, *The Future of the American Family* (Chicago: Moody, 1993), 131.

9. H. Kauffman, "The Case of the Missing Wedding Rings," at www.renewingtheheart.com/articles/A0000056.html (2002), 2, accessed 2 July 2002.

10. L. Minton, "Fresh Voices," *Parade,* 1 March 1998, 12.

11. K. C. Scott, "Mom, I Want to Live with My Boyfriend," *Reader's Digest,* February 1994, 77–80.

12. Jennifer Roback Morse, "Why Not Take Her for a Test-Drive?" http://www.boundless.org/2001/departmentsbeyond_buddies/90000498html (2001), 2, accessed 2 July 2002.

Chapter 5: The Consequences of Cohabiting: The Hard Realities

1. S. L. Brown and A. Booth, "Cohabitation Versus Marriage: A Comparison of Relationship Quality," *Journal of Marriage and the Family* 58 (1996): 668–78.

2. L. L. Bumpass and J. A. Sweet, "Cohabitation, Marriage, and Union Stability: Preliminary Findings from NSFH2," *NSFH Working Paper,* no. 65 (Madison: University of Wisconsin-Madison, Center for Demography and Ecology, 1995).

3. Z. Wu and T. R. Balakrishnan, "Dissolution of Premarital Cohabitation in Canada," *Demography* 32 (1995): 529.

4. L. L. Bumpass and J. A. Sweet, "National Estimates of Cohabitation," *Demography* 26 (1988): 620.

5. Ibid.

6. Wu and Balakrishnan, "Dissolution of Premarital Cohabitation in Canada," 526.

7. Ibid., 621.

8. L. L. Bumpass, J. A. Sweet, and A. Cherlin, "The Role of Cohabitation in Declining Rates of Marriage," *Journal of Marriage and the Family* 53 (1991): 919.

9. Bumpass and Sweet, "Children's Experience in Single Parent Families: Implications of Cohabitation and Marital Transitions," *Family Planning Perspectives* 21 (1989).

10. Ibid., 258–59.

11. David Popenoe and Barbara Defoe Whitehead, "Should We Live Together? What Young Adults Need to Know About Cohabitation Before Marriage," *The National Marriage Project*, January 1999, 3–4.

12. J. Laskin, "The Nevers of Living Together," *Unmarried Couples and the Law*, at www.palimony.com (2002), 1–2, accessed 2 July 2002.

13. R. Deech, "The Case Against the Legal Recognition of Cohabitation," in *Marriage and Cohabitation in Contemporary Societies*, ed. J. M. Eekelaar (Toronto: Butterworths, 1980), 301–2.

14. J. E. Stets and M. A. Strauss, "The Marriage License as a Hitting License: A Comparison of Assaults in Dating, Cohabiting and Married Couples," in *Violence in Dating Relationships*, ed. M. A. Pirog-Good and J. E. Stets (New York: Praeger, 1989), 36–39.

15. Ibid., 47–48.

16. A. DeMaris and W. MacDonald, "Premarital Cohabitation and Marital Instability: A Test of the Unconventionality Hypothesis," *Journal of Marriage and the Family* 55 (1993): 404.

17. P. G. Jackson, "On Living Together Unmarried," *Journal of Family Issues* 4 (1983): 41.

18. P. R. Newcomb, "Cohabitation in America: An Assessment of Consequences," *Journal of Marriage and the Family* 41 (1979): 559.

19. Scott Stanley quoted in Karen S. Peterson, "Cohabiting Can Make Marriage an Iffy Proposition," *USA Today,* 8 July 2002, 2.

20. Ibid., 2.

21. A. Greeley, *Faithful Attraction* (New York: Tom Doherty, 1991), 225.

22. Ibid., 206.

23. E. Thomson and U. Colella, "Cohabitation and Marital Stability: Quality or Commitment," *Journal of Marriage and the Family* 54 (1992): 259.

24. George Barna, *The Future of the American Family* (Chicago: Moody, 1993), 134.

25. Thomson and Colella, "Cohabitation and Marital Stability," 266.

26. A. DeMaris and K. V. Rao, "Premarital Cohabitation and Subsequent Marital Stability in the United States: A Reassessment," *Journal of Marriage and the Family* 54 (1992): 189.

27. Bumpass and Sweet, "National Estimates of Cohabitation," *Demography* 26 (1989): 621.

28. M. A. Lamanna and A. Riedmann, *Marriages and Families: Making Choices and Facing Change* (Belmont, Calif.: Wadsworth, 1994), 219.

29. D. Robb, *Love and Living Together* (Philadelphia: Fortress Press, 1977), 46.

Chapter 6: What Does the Bible Say About Cohabitation?

1. C. Stinnett, "They Live Together and Attend Your Church," *Christianity Today.com* (2002), 1, accessed 20 June 2002.

2. G. D. Fee, *The First Epistle to the Corinthians* (Grand Rapids: Eerdmans, 1987), 196.

3. John MacArthur Jr., *First Corinthians* (Chicago: Moody, 1984), 123.

4. John Calvin, *Commentary of the Epistles of Paul the Apostle to the Corinthians* (Grand Rapids: Baker, 1979), 1:179.

Chapter 7: Marriage as a Covenant in the Bible

1. *NBC Today,* 13 August 1997.
2. *Wall Street Journal,* 18 August 1997.
3. Clarence Page, 22 August 1997. Page's column appears in the *Bloomington-Normal Pantagraph.*
4. G. P. Hugenberger, *Marriage as a Covenant* (Lieden, Netherlands: E. J. Brill, 1994), 171–72.
5. E. Smick, *"berit,"* in *The Theological Wordbook of the Old Testament,* ed. R. Harris (Chicago: Moody, 1980), 1:128.
6. G. J. Botterweck and H. Ringgrin, eds., *The Dictionary of the Old Testament* (Nashville: Abingdon, 1982), 6:260–62.
7. G. E. Mendenhall, "covenant," in *The Interpreter's Dictionary of the Bible,* ed. G. A. Buttrick et al. (Nashville: Abingdon, 1962), 714–23. Mendenhall outlined the kinds and classifications of covenants in the ancient world and connected them to the Bible, taking care to point out their religious and sacred dimension. Subsequent scholarship "picked at" Mendenhall's analysis, but did not successfully overthrow his conclusions.
8. D. T. McCarthy, *Old Testament Covenant* (Richmond, Va.: John Knox Press, 1972), 227.
9. R. Showers, *Lawfully Married* (Langhorne, Pa.: Philadelphia College of the Bible, 1983), 11–16.
10. "Dear Abby," *Bloomington-Normal Pantagraph,* 16 November 2002.

Chapter 8: The Marriage Covenant in Christian History

1. M. A. Fineman and D. S. Clarke, "On Target and Off in 2002," *New York Times,* 28 December 2002.
2. J. E. Grubbs, "Pagan and Christian Marriage: The State of the Question," *Journal of Early Christian Studies* 23 (1994): 381.

3.	Tertullian, "To His Wife," in *Tertullian's Treatises on Marriage and Remarriage,* trans. William P. Le Saint (New York: Newman Press, 1951), 11–12.

4.	J. Chrysostom, "Homily 20 on Ephesians," in *Marriage in the Early Church,* trans. and ed. David G. Hunter (Minneapolis: Fortress Press, 1992), 86–87.

5.	Augustine, *Confessions* (London: Penguin Books, 1984), 72.

6.	J. A. Coleman, *100 Years of Catholic Social Thought* (New York: Maryknoll, 1991), 553.

7.	M. E. Schild, "Marriage Matters in Luther and Erasmus," *The Reformed Theological Review* 39 (1980): 65.

8.	W. Lazareth, *Luther on the Christian Home* (Philadelphia: Muhlenberg Press, 1960), 169.

9.	R. Erlich, "The Teaching of the Reformers on Marriage," *Biblical Theology* 19 (1974): 7.

10.	Lazareth, *Luther on the Christian Home,* 228.

11.	J. Halkett, *Milton and the Idea of Matrimony* (New Haven: Yale University Press, 1970), 1.

12.	M. Savelle, *Seeds of Liberty* (New York: A. A. Knopf, 1948), 27.

13.	William Gouge, *Of Domesticall Duties* (Norwood, N.J.: W. J. Johnson, 1976).

14.	J. T. Johnson, *A Society Ordained by God* (Nashville: Abingdon, 1970), 56.

15.	E. S. Morgan, *The Puritan Family* (Boston: Trustees of the Public Library, 1956), 12.

16.	Ibid.

17.	J. C. Wynn, ed., *Sermons on Marriage and Family Life* (Nashville: Abingdon, 1956), 50–51.

18.	K. Barth, *Church Dogmatics* (Edinburgh: T & T Clarke, 1961), 3:184.

19.	Ibid., 3:144.

20.	Ibid., 3:203.

21.	Ibid., 3:240.

22.	Ibid., 3:206–7.

23. W. J. Everett and W. Johnson, *Blessed Be the Bond* (Landham, Md.: University Press of America, 1990), 7.

24. K. Scott and M. Warren, *Perspectives on Marriage: A Reader* (New York: Oxford University Press, 1993), 104.

25. Ibid.

26. Ibid.

27. Ibid., 105–6.

28. Ibid., 108–9.

29. Ibid., 106.

30. G. Forster, *Marriage Before Marriage* (Bramcote, England: Grove Books, 1988), 7.

31. American Bar Association, *Your Legal Guide to Marriage and Other Relationships,* Public Education Division (Chicago: American Bar Association, 1989), 11.

32. A. Greeley, *Faithful Attraction* (New York: Tom Doherty, 1991), 241.

33. G. L. Dahl, *How Can We Keep Christian Marriages from Falling Apart?* (Nashville: Nelson, 1988).

34. R. Halverson and D. Halverson, "Marriage Built on Covenant," in *Marriage That Works,* ed. A. Augsburger (Scottdale, Pa.: Herald Press, 1984), 50–53.

Chapter 10: Pastoral Counseling with Cohabiting Couples:
Two Key Principles

1. C. Koehl and S. VanGoren, "Marriage on the Cheap," *Newsweek,* 8 January 1996, 8.

2. "Home Town Heroes," *Focus on the Family Citizen,* 21 November 1994, 6.

Chapter 11: Pastoral Counseling with Cohabiting Couples:
Specific Guidelines

1. J. G. Swank Jr., "Church Weddings Are Not for Everyone," *Christianity Today* 20 (1977): 26–27.
2. J. Cymbala and D. Merrill, *Fresh Wind, Fresh Fire* (Grand Rapids: Zondervan, 1997).
3. Ibid., 128–29.

Chapter 12: Pastoral Counseling with Couples Who Have Cohabited

1. R. E. Silverman, "The Upside of Living in Sin," *Wall Street Journal,* 5 March 2003.